THE LIFE OF VICTORY

Eric Guy is a transformational individual and his book is an inspiration for anyone who wants or needs to change his or her life's journey. If you believe people can change, and especially if you don't, this book is a must read. I've known Eric for five years and I've been constantly amazed at his ability to help people see inside themselves and change their self-destructive behavior. He has helped families and organizations learn how to communicate on a much deeper level. This book is the result of years of hard work and experience. It will be an enriching journey for anyone who reads it.

Dick Singer
Best Practice Chair, Master Chair
Vistage International

Eric Guy is not of this world. Neither is his book. In fact, the very idea of overcoming the world's (our environment's) negative effect on us is the point of this book. Through his own life experience, shared with great candor, Eric helps us understand how we become angry and fearful people. More important, how we might gain the skills to turn toward our best self and live a victimless life. I hope to be the first book order—30 copies at least—so that I can share with friends and family who are living the same struggle that Eric and I are. We shall overcome!

Tim McCarthy
Founder and Chief Mission Officer
The Business of Good
and
author of Empty Abundance—Finding Meaning
Through Mindful Giving

Knowing a bit about Eric's life story with regard to who he used to be and who he is today, I know Eric is a model of what personal transformation can do to positively impact the lives of numerous human beings! I've also had the privilege and honor of working with Eric, and the treat of seeing him significantly impact the lives of my Vistage CEO Group members during his inspirational speaker presentation!

Bob Dabic
Master Chair—Orange County
Best Practice Chair—Los Angeles
Vistage International

Eric's book is profoundly simple. The practical principles shared in the book will cause you to take steps to living a champion-filled life influenced by love.

The insights that Eric shares capture your heart and lead you to the desire for victorious living. I just love Eric's transparency and vulnerability; it's refreshing!

Larry Bettencourt
Founding and Lead Pastor
Champion Life Church
Beaver Falls, PA

Working in a family business is extremely gratifying, especially when each family member is aware of the others' skill sets and personalities. It does, however, come with challenges— such as typical family dynamics and personal interaction between family members that can exist when there is disagreement. In order to facilitate a better family dynamic at work, Eric worked with us to not only be able to recognize each of our strengths and how we can complement each other, but also to be able to identify what the real issue is at hand that creates conflict or misunderstandings within the family. We are now able to resolve the issues in a candid but amicable manner. Eric Guy has a calming style which has truly helped the family to love and work together better.

Michael, Jeffrey, Jack, and John Mascaro
Mascaro Construction Company, L.P

THE LIFE
OF
VICTORY

MASTERING THE SECRET OF CHOOSING
LOVE OVER FEAR

By Eric Guy, MSW, LSW

THE LIFE OF VICTORY
Copyright © 2016 by Eric Guy

To contact the author, Eric Guy, visit:

Website ....: www.CenterForVictory.com

Email ....: Eric@CenterForVictory.com

LinkedIn...........: https://www.linkedin.com/in/ericguylsw

Twitter.............: https://twitter.com/center4victory

Facebook........: https://www.facebook.com/CenterforVictory/

YouTube.........: https://www.youtube.com/watch?v=3KArK6Wrk30

Instagram ....: @CenterForVictory

Printed in the United States of America

To contact the publisher, inCredible Messages Press, visit www.inCredibleMessages.com

ISBN 978-0-9908265-4-5 paperback

ISBN 978-0-9908265-5-2 eBook

SELF-HELP / Personal Growth / Happiness

Book coaching: Bonnie Budzowski

Cover design: Bobbie Fox Fratangelo

Acknowledgments

To all those whom I have had the honor and privilege of serving, thank you for all your hard work and proving that we can overcome anything in front of us when we change that which is within us.

To my friends, thank you for letting me be me, and for all the encouragement you give.

To my family, thank you for all the support.

Brother, I think you have always understood me, and you're the only one like me. Thanks.

Mom, thanks for always being on my side, even though sometimes you probably shouldn't have been, and for being my fan.

Dad, thanks for not giving up on me. You are my hero.

To my children, thank you for all the light you bring into my life. Josiah, you inspire me to do the right thing always. Faith, you inspire me to always be happy.

To my wife, Tammy, my regulation, it never gets old with you. Thank you for all your patience and everything you have sacrificed for our family.

CONTENTS

FOREWORD

"Oh, that hair has got to go!"

I'm afraid (and a little ashamed) to admit that this hasty little mental gem represents my first impression of Eric Guy. Long, loose, and free, the pile of hair on my friend's head surely makes an impression upon first glance.

What I've since come to learn, appreciate, and treasure, however, is that the hair not only should remain on Eric's head, but that it needs to. The fact that he grows it long, feels good about it, and lives his life in a state of grace, courage, and comfort—with his hair the most outward and immediate visual proof—also gives people the chance to stop and think:

- "Am I as comfortable in my own skin as this fellow?"

- "What opportunities am I missing, due to apprehension, over-thinking, or fear of embarrassment?"

- "Why wouldn't I want to live in freedom and good-hearted joy, too?"

Eric has this effect on people.

My first meeting with Eric came as the result of an introduction from a mutual friend and business advisor. We sat down in one of those ubiquitous coffee franchises that have become the de facto network for business discussions these days. Over some pricey lattes, the discussion quickly shifted from the usual trite introductory banter into a rich, deep, thought-provoking discussion of personal histories, shared philosophies, and the role of interpersonal relationships in building a successful business and life.

The depth of the conversation shook me a little. It scared me a little. It surprised me a little. And it surpassed any expectation I may have had for this quick get-to-know-you chat.

As I said, Eric has this effect on people. It's why we became partners in business that day, with nothing but success together ever since.

When I founded Predictive Synergistic Systems, the idea that drove the business was that understanding the true skills, interests, and motivators of individuals would serve as reliable guidelines to steer those individuals into the right jobs for organizations. That idea is still the driver. But thanks to Eric's unique gifts, we can now take that basic premise to a higher level of performance and results for our clients.

I've helped Eric understand how to apply analytics from a business perspective. He has helped me understand how each individual figures into the equation—not just regarding where the individual may fall on a chart, but also regarding what that individual may carry in his or her heart. Eric has humanized the data in ways that no piece of software ever could hope to replicate.

This book contains some of the most impactful stories and meaningful guidance you may ever read. Eric comes to these ideas both through his extensive education and, more important, through his first-hand experience. He is no cold, clinical theoretician, statistician, or strategist. He's a 100-percent, boots-on-the-ground, let's-roll-up-our-sleeves-and-get-dirty, and I'm-all-in, coach, counselor, and creative force.

Eric has helped our business, and I have seen him help families and other organizations in the same way, using his talents, skills, and an inexplicable yet inescapable sense of peace that cannot be bottled or marketed. You need to experience this sense to start to get a taste of what I'm trying to describe.

In lieu of that, please trust me in stating unequivocally that the grace, tact, and professionalism of Eric Guy all come pulsing through in the pages to follow. You're lucky to be holding this book in your hands. If you make the most of it, it will help make the most of you.

In what I may only characterize as the highest compliment I can give, Eric reminds me of my own mom. Like her, he is deeply authentic, smart as a whip, with a great sense of humor, and an even greater sense of loving calm. He remains my trusted confidante, my valued business partner, and my treasured friend.

So, yeah. The hair can stay.

Dan Courser
CEO—Predictive Synergistic Systems

Chapter 1

INTRODUCTION:
HOW I GOT FROM THERE TO HERE

Say, here's a question for you: Are you crazy?

Yeah, me too. Most everybody is, at least a little.

If crazy means having a history of thinking and behavior that took a long time to change for the better, we are all crazy. Or if crazy means taking two steps forward and one step backward, instead of making steady progress toward a somewhat fuzzy goal, we fit the definition. Or if crazy means grasping, groping, and guessing as to what our true calling in life may be, we've been there.

No doubt, we're all a little crazy.

This book is all about recognizing the crazy and offering a clear path out of it, into serenity, peace, personal power, and achievement. It's possible to attain all these things. I can vouch for it because I've lived it. I've moved from the crazy to a place of control and balance, and it has made life irrefutably happier, easier, and more satisfying.

Here's a quick run-through to prove the point.

The best characterization of the house in which I grew up may be "angry." The root cause of the anger never clearly manifested itself during my kid years, but that root always felt close by. It was a heavy, unseen, cloying, suffocating presence. Tension, like a humid cloud, crushed its way into every corner of every room, every conversation, and every interaction. This was especially true in the difficult relationship I had with my dad.

It was a tough way to grow up, and the anger spilled and spread like quicksilver into all areas of my life.

I played football in both high school and college. In college, I played with a tight end that put toothpaste in the keyhole of my locker after I didn't invite him to a party. At the next practice, I knocked him cold as he came across the middle of the field for a pass. He never came across the field again while I was there.

I was not the biggest player on the team, but I had worked myself into great shape and loved the high testosterone juices of football. Thanks in part to my growing-up years, I had trouble containing my high level of swagger and intimidation off the field. I enjoyed creating fear as the path to gaining respect for one simple reason. I was so damn good at it.

My high school coaches saw this quality in me, and they constantly challenged—maybe even taunted—me, to get the most out of my aggression on behalf of the team. A favorite challenge of theirs was, "I bet you can't!" To me, this was like giving Popeye a tub of spinach. My response definitely helped us win games, but again, I had no idea of control or balance.

In college, I played on two Division II national championship teams, despite the fact that the head coach and I rarely saw eye-to-eye on anything. The school prided itself on being a conservative campus, yet there I was, sporting two pierced ears and a gaudy bandana. Every aspect of my appearance screamed rebellion.

I did not fit in at all there, to put it mildly, and I nearly flunked out my first semester. Then I found a sociology teacher who let me write out my answers instead of taking multiple-choice tests, a form of standardized testing at which I had never done well. Once I was free to explain myself regarding the course work, my grades shot up to a 3.4 GPA in my second semester.

At last, the clouds had begun to part, even if it was a tiny bit. The constraints and shackles that had clamped down on and around me for so long started to loosen. All of a sudden, the reasons to be angry diminished by a small portion. The openness of that professor to my academic difficulties provided the first foreshadowing of what I do today, seeing how things can come together in new ways to reach new and better conclusions. In no way, though, was I out of the woods.

The process of gaining better control and balance took a monumental leap forward when, later in my college career, I met the girl who was to become my wife. I first saw Tammy at a fraternity party and was immediately attracted to her, even though I didn't learn her name. It took dogged detective work over the next couple of weeks to track Tammy down again, only to have her say she didn't want to go out with me, based in large part on my reputation of a hair-trigger temper.

Tammy relented in time, and we spent our first date watching the Disney movie, *Jungle Book*. I mean, how tame can you get? That year I went on a spring break trip, with Tammy's parting words resounding in my brain, "Don't screw it up, or it's over." That was the worst spring break trip ever. For the first time, I truly did not want to be there. I knew where I wanted—no, needed—to be.

Things changed even more after that. Tammy gave me a jar containing Bible verses and asked me to pick one out every day to read. That exercise further increased my desire to strengthen my connection with her. The timing could not have been better, given that my college football career came crashing to an end due to injuries and subsequent surgery.

While I couldn't play anymore, I realized I could excel at more than football. I enjoyed the social sciences just as much. I became greatly interested in Scripture, too. Still, the lingering essence of anger from my childhood years had not been squelched completely. I evolved intellectually and emotionally to a place where I wanted to work with people, but I wanted the job to be one in which I could still crack heads together if needed, like the DEA or the FBI. Anger proved a most difficult master from which to escape. Control still eluded me.

The big aha moment arrived shortly thereafter when someone nearly took the rear bumper off my truck as I was backing out of a driveway. The guy stopped, leaped from his car, and started giving me a lot of lip for almost causing him to have an accident. Immediately, a flood of adrenaline rushed through me, just as it had in college when I knocked out the tight end coming across the football field. I grabbed this guy and pushed him against my truck. Anger, visceral and violent, nearly reclaimed me.

Over the guy's shoulder, I could see into the front seat of my truck. There, as if positioned purely for this moment, sat a small green devotional I had been using to broaden my spiritual development. Instantly, silently, remorsefully, I released the guy and he drove away.

I changed that day. At long last, I achieved control. The choice had been placed squarely before my eyes, my mind, my heart, my soul. God gave me a sign, and I finally figured out that it was time I listened.

At the time of my aha moment, I was still in college. Although physically incapable of playing football, I was permitted to finish college on scholarship. People, situations, and relationships that did not represent positive influences were removed from my life. I'd go off into the woods alone to walk and think. Now that control had come, the next challenge became achieving balance.

Upon graduation, I did an internship at a full-lockdown facility for juvenile offenders. At the end of that assignment, the director told me, "You have a gift. You don't realize how well you do this. The way you interact with kids is unique." The director wanted me to meet with the dean of social work at the University of Pittsburgh. This led to a summer spent in Georgia working with troubled kids, and then work at a youth camp closer to my western Pennsylvania home.

I came to appreciate that people don't understand why troubled kids are at these places. The kids are not inherently evil. As I took more college courses, I became frustrated that so many book-smart professors expounded ideas and practices that simply would never work in real life—and I knew, because I had worked and been in the system. That frustration would germinate into a passion to do things differently and more effectively, by meeting people where they were in their journey. Balance started to come into a little sharper focus for me.

Tammy and I got married, settled into a home, and became part of the local community. I became a licensed social worker and took a job as a supervisor at a facility providing therapy. My wife had some medical issues and was told she could not bear children; yet, she became pregnant and miscarried. A second pregnancy, though high-risk, came to term. Our first child was born.

Now, my sense of deepening balance began to face a series of tests. After our son came along, I became determined to raise him right, in a home not steeped in anger, but in love and support. In order to do that, I could not leave him with anyone else to watch, so I worked out a deal with my employer to come in during afternoons, once my wife came home from teaching school.

I found that, working alone, I could get more work done at better quality, but my employer eventually disagreed and we parted ways. With one baby in the house and soon another on the way, I got my securities license and began selling investments. Here again, balance was tested, as my wife suffered a stroke during her second trimester.

Tammy carried the baby to term again, giving birth to our daughter just prior to the 9-11 attacks. With the stock market in turmoil, I shucked the short-hair, suit-and-tie restraints of traditional investment selling, and—just as with the earrings and bandana on the college football team—I reverted to what worked best for me. With long hair and casual clothes, I achieved just as much success—even more—as before.

Still, questions pestered and lingered. The big questions, like these: What am I doing? Why am I doing it? Is this where I belong? Why am I not happy? What needs to change, and how? These were the questions essential to achieving balance.

Answering the questions led me to resign from the world of securities. The investment firm flew in a top executive to convince me to stay, but I walked away, taking a job working midnight shift at a psychiatric hospital. During the day, I stayed home and took care of the family.

The next test came soon after. Tammy had a second stroke, causing paralysis on one side of her body. Our response to that test came without debate or discussion. We moved back home to be near a wider, deeper, and stronger support system.

The quest for balance continued, as I started looking for another way. I began seeing things, putting things together, thinking differently about relationships and complete health for people. I had continuing conversations with God, having learned that the spiritual is just as important—perhaps even more so—than the intellectual, physical, and emotional parts of each of us.

We did what we needed to do to keep Tammy healthy, but there was much more to her situation than the physicality of it. What about her mind, her spirit? Drawing from her experience, along with everything I had lived through to that point, I just knew there was a different way to treat people, seeing how Scripture fits with science and psychology. Within a year, my world exploded in a positive way when a call came from an old friend on the speaking circuit, and I began spreading the word about control and balance to audiences worldwide.

Here's what it all comes down to: Everything is about relationships—you must get centered and connected to get it done, whatever "it" may be.

We're born into a place of abundance with unbounded love, but we are raised into poverty to concentrate on what we lack. Let's recalibrate that equation. For goodness sake, I have met people living in tents in Africa who are happy, and I have met people who get upset because they'll only make $600,000 this year instead of $800,000.

We've taken everything that's simple and made it complex. Why? That's crazy! We don't need to be crazy, not even a little bit.

Keep it simple, do the right things, and everything else will fall into line. When it's all aligned, it flows. You can do anything when the stress is gone. Use your gifts to empower yourself and those around you. Each of us has this capability within us. When all concentric circles in your life provide comfort, that comfort radiates back out.

Control and balance. It is attainable. Shake loose from the crazy. Read on, and learn more.

--------- Chapter 2 ---------

WE'RE DOING EVERYTHING BACKWARDS

Chopper Dude was having none of it.

During a session with a local group where I was offering my views on relationships, balance, and how to build a happy life, one member of the class simply rejected virtually every concept I had, every suggestion I made, every word I uttered.

Large, muscular, tattooed to the hilt, and draped all in leather, the Harley-riding Chopper Dude cut an imposing figure. I may have played football in my day, but even by those standards, this fellow had the intimidation factor down pat.

My intern was with me at this particular evening's event. Tiny, petite, and a little nervous even on a good day, she stood in quaking, fearful awe of Chopper Dude. When he interrupted me, mid-lecture, I thought my intern might pass out on the spot.

"This is bullshit!" he all but shouted, standing up and pointing a finger in my face.

"Well, I'm sorry you feel that way, but I respect your thoughts and invite you to stay with me a little longer," I replied, concentrating to keep my voice level

and my emotions in check. "I'm glad you're here. Please stay and hear me out, and I would be happy to talk more with you one-to-one afterward."

Chopper Dude gave me a look that seemed to blend confusion, anger, frustration, and respect, all within a three-second span. He sat down again, remaining for the rest of the evening's class.

After the room had emptied and everyone had left, my intern and I were packing things up when we looked out into the parking lot and saw Chopper Dude still there, leaning against his enormous motorcycle, staring back at us through the window. Now I got a little scared. Not nearly as badly as my intern, mind you, but scared nonetheless.

He ambled back into the building, back into the room where our class had been conducted and closed the door behind him. We just looked at each other for what seemed an interminable amount of time. Then, just as I was about to speak, the most amazing thing happened. Something neither my intern nor I ever saw coming.

Chopper Dude began to cry.

I mean he wept like he had never wept before. Between gasping sobs, he tried to tell us what had affected him so deeply that evening. In time, as he gained control of himself, it became clear.

"I never had somebody not judge me for what I thought before," he said.

For his entire 40-something life, this dude's feelings and thoughts had been consistently devalued.

Rejected. Dismissed. Stamped as unimportant, unworthy, and unimpressive.

Parents, teachers, bosses, and peers had nearly destroyed this man's entire sense of self-worth—because they never appreciated his starting point.

The place where his value truly rested.

They were doing everything backward.

As a society, we're going backward. From the cradle to the grave, we start interacting with other people from the wrong end of the spectrum. This leads to some tremendous problems.

Most of us have been taught that we can change our lives by thinking differently. We start from the premise that change begins by applying logic—and that's what's wrong.

Change begins not with the conscious mind, the logical mind, the quick-fix mind, or the do-it-yourself mind. You can't just read the *Life for Dummies* and do the recommended steps. That's the wrong end at which to start.

No, change truly and only can begin with the unconscious mind, the mind that defers to the more basic—meaning the place that serves as the base, the foundation, of everything else—part of our being. The place people call the "gut."

To achieve lasting, meaningful, tangible change toward greater balance and happiness in your life, you have to deal with this unconscious level first. This is where a lifetime of negative conditioning must be reversed.

The fact is, we react at an unconscious, cellular level before our minds realize it. Science has begun to validate the connections between emotions, cell behavior, and physical health. When your emotional health improves, so does your physical health.

Our problem as a society, however, is that we continue the inversion of how to build and maintain emotional health. We keep doing things backward. In other words, we keep applying conscious logic first when the true portal can only be found at the unconscious emotional level.

You must decide where your foundation rests: somewhere on the spectrum of Love on one end and Fear on the other. Only then can you try to apply logic and intellect.

Anybody can get a book or a CD to "tell you what to do," but that doesn't take into consideration any of the root causes and motivations for behavior, which can all be found in the unconscious. To use logic as the starting point toward finding balance and peace is to start at the end.

One summer afternoon, I took my son and a bunch of his buddies to our local amusement park for a day of fun. One of the kids, whom I knew to be fearless on the sports field, was terrified of roller coasters. It seemed such an anomaly to me, but his fear was real. There was no way on God's green earth that any of his friends or I was going to "talk him into" not being afraid of roller coasters.

Appeals to a logical explanation of safety precautions, the fun factor involved, or any other checklist of wonderful at-tributes about roller coasters held no water for this young fellow. Roller coasters scared him at an elemental level, and he wasn't going to set foot on one. Case closed.

We respond to situations unconsciously first, because stress causes a reaction. Stress causes distorted thinking and blinds short-term thinking. For example, after a four-year-old pulls a tablecloth to the floor, breaking your best china, you may ask him, "Why did you do that?" Veteran parents know the most likely answer is, "I don't know."

Well, guess what? The kid really doesn't know! You're asking him a logical, conscious-level question, when he had been acting based purely on an emotional, unconscious-level gut impulse. There is no logical reason to pull a tablecloth off a table set for dinner.

Asking for a logical explanation is starting at the wrong end. The answer lies somewhere much deeper than that. The child has an unmet need—whether it's for information, to satisfy his curiosity, to guarantee some parental attention, or another fundamental reason. It rests at the emotional, unconscious level.

So, how can this unconscious level be probed, explained, and understood? The answer is both simple and unbelievably complex. Everything we do is about relationships. When stressed, we cannot bond with other people. Stress affects our ability to function, even our health.

The more you regress in your relationships due to stress, the less logical you become. On the flip side, though, as your relationships enjoy minimal stress, the bonds become easier to establish and strengthen. Every part of your mind functions at a more optimal and optimized level of performance.

Think of it this way. Every New Year's Eve, we set resolutions for the coming year. Things we want to accomplish, steps we want to take to improve ourselves. We know how to set our goals intellectually. That's easy. But what stops us from achieving those goals? Why do we end up making the same New Year's resolutions year after year?

I contend it's because everything comes back to relationships. Declaring the intellectual, logic-based "what" of your intended goals may be easy. Fully appreciating the deeper, emotion-based "why" behind your goals is more difficult. Yet that's where success begins.

For example, most people say they want to lose weight. Great, that's a worthy goal. But why do you want to lose weight? To be healthier? Okay, but go deeper. To live longer? Yes, but go deeper still. To be with your children and their children? Now we're getting warm. Where is the real, true "why" behind your intentions? Get to that answer, and you begin to turn your life toward the positive, toward a balance that can bring happiness and peace.

When asked what surprised him the most, the Dalai Lama said,

> *Man, because he sacrifices his health in order to make money. Then he sacrifices money to recuperate his health. And then he is so anxious about the future that he does not enjoy the present; the result being that he does not live in the present or the future. He lives as if he is never going to die, and then he dies having never really lived.*

Too much thinking, not enough feeling. Doing everything backward. Here's the fact. We are hardwired to connect with each other. We are built for relationships. Everything in our makeup, right down to the cellular level, rests, resides, and relishes in building as many healthy, positive relationships as we can. It is the true key to life.

Sadly, however, many people need emotional Ex-lax®. They need to get emotionally regulated. I like to think of the term "emotion" as a contraction that actually means "energy in motion." Emotion drives our perception of life, our decision-making, and ultimately the level of balance and peace we achieve.

As I stated earlier, we all operate at this basic, unconscious, emotional level somewhere on the spectrum between Love and Fear. Here is a list of what each starting point brings to our lives:

LOVE	FEAR
Internal Motivation	External Motivation
Influence	Control
Abundance	Scarcity
Spirit	Ego
Thriving	Surviving

It's probably safe to say that most people would prefer the life influences that reside on the Love side of this ledger. We are made to live in abundance. This is the message of Scripture. When you take your influence from the world (Fear) and not the spirit (Love), life becomes more difficult.

Even in this disoriented world, those who live based on Love and the spirit find that it's a little scary because everybody else is running around so messed up and Fear-based. This distinction is so important that I will begin the words "Love" and "Fear" with capital letters throughout this book.

The good news is that you have nothing to be afraid of, that you have been made in the image of God. This is true, even if you were not conditioned to accept and inculcate that.

Each of us needs to understand and get it right, way down inside, that every person writes the rulebook of his or her life. Everybody wants, deserves, and was created to be happy. Most of us aren't happy because we have been misguided. But when a person witnesses an example of how that happiness can be achieved—as Chopper Dude did that one night—it can be life-changing.

I know this to be true at a personal level, thanks to the connection I enjoyed with my grandmother. In my early years, I was scarred by difficult relationships that had built barriers to personal peace. My default reaction to stress had become anger and violence, but that sort of response never entered my mind when I interacted with my grandmother.

Why? Because she saw me for the person I really was. She set an example of tolerance, respect, and Love. She wrote to me every week, especially when I was in college. She never condemned me or made me feel like my opinions and decisions were anything to be ashamed of or ridiculed.

I didn't listen to anybody else when I was a teenager, but I hung on my grandmother's every word. She wasn't afraid of me, like so many other people were at that time, because we had a loving connection, a healthy and positive relationship. I wanted to be in her presence. I took time to be around her. I wanted to do what was right in her eyes. The frail, gentle, wrinkled old lady who loved me unconditionally made a monumental difference in my life. I still feel her presence deep in my bones, even today.

My grandmother operated from a foundation of Love. Her life had plenty of hardship, injustice, sadness, and struggle. But when a person's unconscious rests on a platform of Love, not Fear, relationships can still flower and bloom. Conversely, a Fear-based foundation shuts out trust and relationship building.

My grandmother could also discipline me when no one else could. This flowed from a foundation of Love, as well, because true discipline has nothing to do with Fear. Look carefully at the word itself to find out why. To "discipline" means to create a disciple, to guide, like a shepherd's crook— not to hit, but to guide.

Bad behavior is not logic-based; it comes from an unmet need. Remember the four-year-old pulling down the table-cloth?

You've probably heard the Bible verse, "Spare the rod and spoil the child." Like the shepherd's crook, we've taken this piece of Scripture out of context, as well, because of our Fear-based mentality. The "rod" in this verse does not describe a paddle, but a guide.

Great leaders don't lead through Fear. Great leaders lead through camaraderie, through an unconscious understanding based on relationships and Love. This principle works the same for leaders of corporations, churches, non-profits, families, and any system of people.

Create the proper Love-based environment for healing, and healing will occur. I once was asked to work with a family from an affluent neighborhood. This family did not lack for comfort or financial security. But a son, a junior in high school at the time, had sunk into a depression. A formerly high-achieving student, in both academics and extracurricular activities, refused to get out of bed or leave his room.

As I worked with the family, I spent the majority of my time with the parents. They needed to create a space for their son to heal. They needed to stop applying logical, intellectual arguments, and a conscious-level approach to the situation, and realize that an unmet need had metastasized to a paralyzing degree in the son's mind.

With careful guidance, the family began to heal. In time, the son returned to school, attended a private college, and earned a 3.9 GPA. He had moved from a Fear-based platform to a Love-based platform, with the support and encouragement of his parents. He regained the relationships to bring his life back into balance and peace.

I like to say that "ego" is an acronym for "Exiting God's Order." We keep eating the apple, which creates Fear. We have been conditioned to run toward Fear. You can pull out all that stuff in the bottom drawer of your life, the stuff that's fed into this Fear-based culture and into your mind and heart, and examine it. You need to get rid of that emotional contagion to move into healthy relationships based on Love.

Know yourself, know your own Fear. Get back into relationships, back into Love.

Our very being, the reason we were created, places relationships at the center. The farther away we get from that center, the more Fear takes over our lives.

The only way to take control is to relinquish control. This is the core message of the Bible, and it's stated over and over:

God is love.

Abide in me and I will abide in you.

Love is patient, love is kind. Love never fails.

Let's stop doing things backward and start appreciating, respecting, and celebrating our unconscious, emotion-based source of person-to-person understanding. Let's move toward a foundation of relationships based on Love, not Fear.

Chapter 3

WHAT'S YOUR STORY?

James looked like a cornered animal. Wild-eyed, desperate, a hair-trigger away from exploding in a rage of vicious self-defense.

When calm and standing erect, James looked like a college linebacker. Huge, tall, solidly built, but only 14 years old. Carrying that heft at 14 may have been physically possible for James, but he also harbored a much heavier burden that proved not so easily carried.

That burden came in the form of a story of neglect, abuse, and misunderstanding—a story that began the day James was born, with chapter after chapter of the same negative story piling up with each successive year of his young life.

James had become a tinderbox, and too many people around him liked playing with matches to see how big his next fireball could blow. His story mattered nothing to them. In their eyes, James was a joke, a potentially dangerous and violent joke, and provoking him had become a favorite form of sport, like poking a bear with a stick to see what will happen.

One day, at the juvenile detention center where I worked as a therapist, James had been having a particularly challenging time of it. He had begun to erupt, first verbally and then physically, from the taunts hurled at him.

On this particular day, the taunts didn't stop after James lashed out. The taunts escalated—so much so that, eventually, four staff members corralled James into a separate room. Their goal was to administer a shot to sedate James. Like an animal in the wild.

James and I had held some interesting conversations prior to all of this excitement. It had taken a long time and a slow brick-by-brick process to build a bridge of trust with him because no one had ever taken that level of interest before. The adults throughout James' life reinforced the negativity of his story by taking no interest in what his story was in the first place.

How and why I ended up entering that secured room that day, I couldn't say. Fate, timing, divine providence—who knows? Yet there I was, facing what could only be described as a street fight, four adults against a terrified 14-year-old.

James turned his head in my direction. His wild, frantic eyes caught sight of me, standing in place, looking directly back at him.

Finding strength he hadn't mustered to that point, James threw off the holds that the four staff members had on him and started to run at me full speed, eyes still blazing.

To see a 6-foot, 200-pound, muscle-bound, adrenaline-soaked young man charging straight at me was quite a memorable experience. I felt sure James would knock me into the wall on his way to the door and freedom.

But I was wrong. I had forgotten that James knew that I knew his story. That he could share things with me. That he trusted me. I should have remembered all that, too.

James, dripping with sweat, heart pounding, breathing heavily, ran until stopping six inches from my face. Stood there for two seconds. Got the confirmation he needed that he could still trust me. And hugged me for all I was worth, sobbing into my shoulder.

You want to see looks of complete dumbfounded speechlessness? You could have seen it on the faces of the four guys who, seconds earlier, were wrestling this kid to the ground to inject him with a sedative. They could not believe their eyes. What happened to transform this crazed animal into a sobbing child so quickly?

All it took was someone willing to understand another person's story, and to help that person turn his story around.

We all have triggers. People push our buttons because those triggers are there, and because they know they can. If you respond to those triggers too long without turning things around, that will become your story.

But it doesn't have to remain your story. No one can make you feel bad, inferior, stupid, inadequate, unwanted, disrespected, or unloved without your permission. We are not born angry or depressed. It all depends on the story we allow to form inside our-

selves—and our willingness to change that story into something more positive.

What's your story? Why are you here?

During our formative years, and even into adulthood and the workplace, we typically hear things like, "You're not able. You can't understand this. You can't accomplish this task satisfactorily." We grow up with a story of lack, shortcoming, failure.

We're told continuously that we need to be something different, something better than what we are or can realistically be expected to achieve. Schools teach that we need to be good at everything. That's a lie.

Why does a child whose natural talent, whose very DNA, heavily favors verbal skills like writing, reading, providing analysis of stated ideas and positions, be held to the highest standards in math and science? An "A" in the one area of study is not the same as an "A" in the other. It does not require the same level of effort or natural interest.

Yet when a child struggles with a subject that is not a natural strength, the child gets a message that he or she isn't measuring up. It builds into and cements a story of under achievement, unworthiness, and failure. It paints us all as victims to one degree or another.

The fact is, you only have to be great at one thing—the thing you love to do and that you do the best. This is a simple concept to state but a tough one to implement and make stick. You can reach peace with this, but you first have to realize how strongly the odds are stacked against this occurring.

Our society can be so strange, even illogical. The story of victimhood we heap upon our kids and each other lingers and festers until it ultimately becomes your story in your mind—a story that takes determined effort and help to escape, clearing the way for a new, more positive and accurate story to appear.

We've all heard of people who suffer true physical and emotional abuse, then somehow escape it, but end up back in new relationships where the same behaviors come around again to hurt them as before. Why do people get stuck in these same cycles? Any logical assessment would say to get out of there and stay out, but the victim mentality becomes engrained and imprinted emotionally.

The nickname of a verbose teenager whose behavior, language, and record of lashing out got him institutionalized, where he was regularly restrained, was Preacher. As a therapist, I got tired of dealing with this situation. It reached the point where, finally, I decided I wasn't willing to wrestle with Preacher and risk getting hurt. I said to Preacher one day, "If you want to be restrained, just get on the ground yourself"— and he did, without another word said.

No physical contact, no struggle, no battling, or grappling. Preacher had been conditioned to associate restraint with connection to another person who might care to hear, contemplate, understand, and act with compassion based on his story. All I had to do was suggest it, and he complied. It was stunning.

All Preacher wanted was connection. The only way he knew to get it was to act out. We went through this unusual process two or three more times until we arrived at a place where we could talk calmly, sitting down, like regular people.

Conditional Love can never measure up completely. It suggests and points to a life of struggle—built on a false premise—that only leads to more problems. We create drama where none exists. We sit and watch the news on TV, then extrapolate the chaos and mayhem shown in between the commercials, coming to the ridiculous conclusion that "It's happening everywhere!"

We have the tendency to roll in sorrow, carrying our troubles into every relationship. All that means is that our mess becomes our message, unless we have the foresight and fortitude to break free.

Take Nelson Mandela, for example. Here was a man imprisoned in South Africa unjustly for decades. He had every reason to become bitter, to become steeped in resentment and hate, and to plot revenge and retaliation should he ever be released. Instead, Mandela let his story create a space for greater peace and Love, not only earning his freedom but also becoming the president of the nation that subjected him to its worst side.

Your story, and how you choose to ingrain it in your mind and heart, can make you bitter or make you better.

Oprah Winfrey offers another example. She had been abused sexually as a child, suffering those particularly painful emotional scars for years. Oprah could be sitting on a couch somewhere in public housing today, soaking up medication, and that would be understandable. Instead, her story has become her glory. Oprah rose above her prior story to write one so much more positive—not only for her personally, but for thousands of people who have benefited from her philanthropic activities as well.

I've heard that the brain acts like Velcro® when it comes to negative stories and occurrences, and like Teflon® regarding positives. The bad stuff sticks, in other words, and the good stuff slides right off. That's human nature, I suppose. The key lies in turning that ratio around to favor the positives.

People are so afraid to encounter themselves—to understand their story and use it for good. It requires a conscious effort to wake up and do it every day, whether you want to or not. I contend that when you don't make this effort consistently, you cheat yourself and others.

Here's a question that may help place all of this into context: Are your relationships unconsciously competitive or consciously complementary? Let me explain my terms. If we are unconsciously competitive in our relationships, it means that in some corner of our minds we are always judging ourselves against the other person. This is a recipe for friction and issues in any relationship. But a consciously complementary relationship actively looks for ways to affirm and accept the other person. It finds the best parts of the other person's story to celebrate.

Here's the big secret to your (and every person's) story: You have the story of champion inside. Yes, I believe and declare that everybody is a champion. Every single person ever. As Scripture says, each of us is "fearfully and wonderfully made." The key comes in what we do with that great gift.

How can you use that story you were told growing up—that story of lack and negativity, never quite measuring up, and failure—to change and use it now for a better viewpoint, a better life? That negative story does not need to be ignored or dismissed entirely. There may be important lessons gleaned there. The story also can be leveraged to serve as the platform for something better. Yeah, been there done that—now, what do you do with it moving outward and upward?

We all have a story of victory. Many of us choose not to use it. It's easier to stand in line for a check than to work. It's easier to hire a lawyer when you spill hot coffee on yourself than to take personal responsibility. Do we succumb to what society tells us to expect and choose, or do we correct it, do we make it better?

We give people permission to abuse us through our stories. Negative and Fear-based, or positive and resting on a mutual respect based on Love—the choice always is ours.

When you react to abuse, you take responsibility for the other person's actions. Even new parents succumb to this without perhaps even realizing it. When a first-time mother lets a three-year-old cause her to react emotionally, it's actually an instance of role reversal. The adult has become the child and the kid has become the adult, because the mother has given the three-year-old permission to abuse her. That's the wrong story for both people in this equation.

College freshmen get into trouble because they're looking for connections, having become unmoored from the safety of their homes and school friends over the past 18 years. Bad connections lead to poor decisions and potentially dangerous situations. Good connections lead to greater unconscious accountability and maturity.

I worked with a family in which one of the children stood out as a great student in high school. He grew up in a very rule-based household, with lots of inflexible stipulations and harshly meted-out consequences. This star student left for college and promptly flunked out. Many years later, he remains seriously underemployed.

What happened? How did his story fail him? Why did he fail to launch into a successful college career after seemingly achieving so much in high school?

It happened because his story was too Fear-based, too control-based, too condition-based, and not built on the firm foundation of unconditional Love.

Think about your own relationships. Do you enable or empower people? To enable means to perpetuate the person's existing story. To empower means to give the person the space to grow and change for the better. You know, we are not born angry or spiteful or resentful. We can be unconditionally in Love with anyone we choose.

Too often, we simply choose not to.

We borrow negative stories and carry them with us the rest of our lives, unless we turn them around to build the true story of a champion. Our story should be one of abundance, thriving—not, "Woe is me." The Bible says, "Give, and it will be given to you. A good measure, pressed down, shaken together and running over, will be poured into your lap. For with the measure you use, it will be measured to you."

We've made life this hugely complex thing, and it's not. Everything's okay—always. We need to challenge the paradigm of negativity and Fear, because the truth is that you're always okay, no matter what.

When Barbie Thomas, at the tender age of 2, lost both arms after mistakenly grabbing the wires of a transformer near her Texas home 35 years ago, her mother decided that neither of them would ever fold, give up, nor take the easy way out of any situation.

"I was not allowed to be negative and say I can't do something," Thomas told *Good Morning America*. "I was always taught to focus on what I can do, not what I can't do." That advice may sound oversimplified. Unattainable. Borderline delusional. Pollyannaish. You may say to yourself, "Who lives like that? Who can sustain such an attitude over the course of a lifetime?"

There's a difference between perpetually and foolishly wearing rose-colored glasses versus making a reasoned choice to acknowledge the positive side of any situation and pursuing it as your true story.

The choice always exists. You can always choose to go positive or negative. Once you realize how you are "wired" subconsciously, you can consciously choose the direction in which you want to go. With the choice to go positive, you place your life immediately on the path toward greater health, balance, and peace. It may not be the easiest process in the world, but it absolutely is the most rewarding.

Barbie Thomas would agree. This real-life Venus de Milo, this mother of two teenage sons, contends at the national level as a fitness competitor—a form of athletic dance and conditioning. What's more, she has placed in the top five nationally and earned the first-ever Inspiration Award from the National Physique Committee.

"We all have our own stuff to deal with," she said. "Mine are just more visible. I survived because God saw the bigger picture and had plans for me."

Barbie Thomas—and her mother before her—knew the intrinsic value of creating and promoting a positive story for yourself, then believing it and acting on it as the basis of building a quality life with Love at its foundation.

What you think about is what you become. No one says it will be easy. Once you decide to change from the negative to the positive, it can radically take you out of your comfort zone. But there's no growth without some pain and effort. Growth will come, even if you don't see it. A woman who is four months pregnant still shows little outward signs of anything different, but she knows that something very different is on its way. The labor pains of birth are terrible, but once it's over, beauty results.

Everything has a gestation period. People may prefer to hold on to the pain and drama in their lives—some would say choosing the devil you know—rather than expand and grow. But there can't be an Easter Sunday of boundless joy and hope without first a Good Friday of pain, sorrow, and testing.

Your story is one of a champion. Your story is one of a victor, not a victim. Once you're aware of the sources of your story, you can choose to change it.

Chapter 4

RELATIONSHIPS AND REGULATION

Kevin had it all.

A child of privilege, he grew up in a home where wealth and security were never a concern. Both existed in abundance. Kevin attended one of the best—if not the best—school districts in the region, and he received a quality education that prepared him well for college and beyond. His father had become quite successful, and the family reaped the rewards of that success in money, comfort, and status.

By all outward appearances, then, Kevin had it all. But he wanted more. So he took it. Over and over and over, in the form of shoplifting.

When out with his high school buddies, Kevin never left a store without taking something he hadn't paid for. These were usually small, unnoticed things: a pack of gum, a set of pens, a CD or DVD.

Everyone knew Kevin could easily afford these items. He could buy a dozen of whatever he pilfered on any given day and never miss the money.

What happened after Kevin stole the stuff made even less sense. Once he successfully got outside with the shoplifted item, Kevin would immediately throw it away. His thievery had no practical purpose. He stole because of the feeling it gave him, not because he intended to use anything he had stolen.

As you might expect of high school boys, Kevin's friends thought his larcenous lunacy was hysterical. It never fully dawned on any of his friends that Kevin's activity might signal a deeper problem, something to be concerned about, or a reason to challenge him about it.

That is, until the day Kevin walked out of an office supply store with a newly stolen stapler—and not just any desktop stapler, but an industrial-sized, cast-metal unit that could staple 50 sheets of paper at once. This stapler weighed multiple pounds.

Then Kevin tossed the stapler into a garbage can.

That was finally enough to cause a group of teenage boys to stop, open-mouthed, and say to Kevin, "Dude, what is up with you? Why do you always do stuff like that?"

Kevin tried to laugh it off, and in time, the boys found other distractions and forgot the strange stapler incident. But the questions stuck in Kevin's mind.

What was up with him? Why was he constantly, recklessly, and unnecessarily pushing his luck?

The answers came, in time. They all revolved around a central truth in Kevin's life. Yes, he had a financially secure home and family life. Financially secure, but not emotionally secure.

As a result, Kevin had turned to his gang of buddies for validation and emotional security. To achieve this, however, Kevin felt the need to ramp up his performance with them. To find a level of border-pushing behavior and the resulting positive feedback that provided a sense of being accepted and valued.

Shoplifting and then nonchalantly throwing the stuff away made him feel good, soothed, validated, and regulated, because of the reaction it always generated from his friends. That emotional high proved fleeting, fading like a chalk picture on a rainy sidewalk with each new episode.

So the stakes had to get ever higher, ever more dangerous, and ever more outrageous, which culminated with stealing the weighty stapler.

When his friends didn't react in the same positive way they always had before, Kevin heard something pop in his mind. The party was over. He had to find a new, better, safer, more secure, and more positive way to get emotionally regulated.

Before he lost it all.

In many of my workshops, I ask participants to list three things they want in life, both personally and professionally. Regardless of the answers I get—losing weight, having a better relationship with a spouse, enjoying more satisfaction at the workplace, and so on—they all have a common theme.

They all tie back to relationships if you look deep enough. We want to lose weight to improve our physical health. We want to have better physical health to live longer. We want to live longer because we want to see our children grow and to someday enjoy our grandchildren. Ultimately, then, we want to lose weight because we Love our family. The root cause of any desire or goal—when you drill deep enough—always rests with the need for better relationships.

Yet satisfying that need requires knowledge and effort. How so? Well, because in any relationship we bring our own blueprints to it. In other words, I don't see the world as it is, I see it through the prism of my experiences and story, and so do you. Healthy relationships require a willingness to understand the other person's needs and blueprints. The good news is that we are designed biologically for connection with other people.

Scripture backs this idea up. The whole New Testament, in fact, carries a consistent message of connection. "Remain in me and I will remain in you," as Christ put it.

So why would we be destined for healthy relationships?

Because relationship produces regulation. Balance.

Predictability. Health. Peace.

Sound good? Of course. Easier said than accomplished or maintained, though.

Research says being dysregulated is at the root of mental disorders. When we're dysregulated, we're fundamentally at risk. Being stressed out does crazy things to the mind. What we really need is connection and regulation.

We have only two means to achieve regulation— relationships and behavior. Any negative behavior is due to dysregulation. Kids want to do what's right and are continuously looking for connection. When those young people go away to college, if they have only had hard and externally-driven regulation imposed on them their whole lives— regulation that now has been suddenly cut off—they may try to regulate themselves through drugs, alcohol, sex, or a combination of all three.

Everything rests on healthy relationships, but people make the mistake of putting conditions on relationships. We tell our children that they need to get good grades, but they hear that unless they measure up we will withhold our Love and approval. The real issue isn't behavior, it is dysregulation and disconnection.

Imposing conditions and qualifiers on relationships leads us to mask our pain, or to kids acting out. We've taught ourselves to do these unhealthy things by setting up structures and restrictions. If you must obey a set of rules for me to like you, a natural underpinning of Fear and anxiety is beneath the relationship. Why can't we use the fallback position that says I will like you no matter what happens and we will see this through together?

To prove the point that most people operate from a Fear-based foundation instead of a Love-based one, I occasionally conduct an exercise in my workshops that intentionally invokes a physiological stress reaction. I ask participants to make and maintain eye contact with a stranger in the room. This usually results in some nervous laughter, as might be expected. Next, I say that you need to be 100% in Love with that person. The stress levels get higher, and the laughter decreases. The tension in the room becomes palpable. When, after a few seconds of this, I tell everyone to turn around again, an immediate wave of relief breaks across the room.

What's happens in this exercise? Why, when the thought of totally loving another person is introduced, do people tense up? It comes back to the destructive nature of stress. Stress means you can't think rationally. You can't function properly. The possibility of establishing a healthy relationship is gone.

When you're really connected, regulated, and operating from a Love-based platform, you are productive. You can think and remember things. You behave in a mature way, able to relate to other people. When you are feeling connected, you realize you are okay.

Healthy relationships depend on mutual understanding and respect. There's a story of a very old Guru. People stood in line to ask him their deepest questions. A mother and her child finally got to the front of the line, and the mother asked, "Guru, can you help my son to stop eating candy?"

The Guru said to come back in two weeks. They came back after two weeks, stood in the long line again, and made it to the front. The woman asked again, "Guru, can you help my son stop eating candy?"

The Guru replied, "Young man, stop eating candy." Incredulous, the woman shrieked, "That's it? That's all you have to say? I could have done that!"

The Guru calmly said, "I had to stop eating candy myself before I could ask someone else to do it."

When relationships are mutual, they go much more smoothly. Building mutual relationships, though, means that both parties take responsibility. For example, parents need to regulate themselves enough to stop reacting to a child who is acting out, and to put the child in a place where he can regulate himself.

I referenced my grandmother in a previous chapter. She didn't react to me—she made suggestions—but I listened to what she had to say because she gave me the space to process and get into balance myself. She continuously, although silently, conveyed the message to me that, "I'll make what's important to you important to me, too." That made all the difference and ensured that our relationship always remained healthy.

Healthy relationships incorporate a mutual awareness of what will be challenging for the other person, as well as for you. When you honestly take full responsibility for a relationship, each person becomes invested thoroughly in the other.

As this happens, the relationship begins to take responsibility for itself, and starts to heal. It becomes a *response-able* relationship, where each person welcomes and embraces the opportunity to support and build up the other. It becomes the manifestation of what Scripture calls the Kingdom of God, where all people live with the purpose and function of helping each other, without expectation of repayment or recognition.

One of the great riddles of life is that even though we are hardwired to Love each other, acting on that impulse is an enormous challenge. A great first step is to look at our own blueprints about others—the assumptions and opinions we have formed around individuals and groups. Most of these assumptions and opinions are, if not outright wrong, at least less than completely accurate.

Try to see someone else's blueprint, not your own. If you can communicate from the other's perspective, listen without rebutting, and stay in communication with the other person, then you can begin to climb out of the Fear-based mentality to create something genuine. Most of our troubles stem from differing blueprints and the resulting misunderstandings.

Are you complementary or competitive? Being complementary means consciously making the whole greater than the sum of its parts. Complementary relationships yield two winners, each with greater balance and regulation. Being competitive, on the other hand, happens unconsciously if we don't communicate from that place of mutual respect. In a competitive relationship, there's a winner and a loser. In a truly healthy relationship, no one loses.

Getting connected means getting into balance, into regulation, and into healthy relationships. At our retreats, we have seen it time and again that when Fear is taken out of the room, no one wants to leave. People realize this is how life is supposed to be, working from a platform of Love, and the revelation is absolutely liberating.

Our modern life puts relationships on the shelf, to our detriment. But the building blocks of turning away from Fear and toward Love remain right in front of us.

Christ said, "Apart from me you can do nothing." He was talking about the need for healthy relationships based on Love. We can live this way and be happy and fulfilled both within ourselves and in relationship with each other. All it takes is the proper thinking and a willingness to regulate ourselves in peace, balance, and Love.

---- Chapter 5 ----

ESCAPING THE VICTIM MENTALITY

Herb lives in a pressure cooker.

And what's worse, he likes it in there.

Herb feels continuous pressure and anxiety, most of it self-induced, self-promoted, and self-centered. He professes to everyone that he truly wants to cultivate meaningful relationships, but everything he does pushes people away instead.

Don't believe him? Herb would be happy to tell you his sad story.

He has so much to deal with at work. His boss is a monster. His co-workers are incompetent. He can't get ahead because the system is stacked against him, even though he's the only one there who knows what he's doing. It regularly falls to him to save everybody else's bacon. Naturally, he gets no support from his wife or kids, who only see him as a meal ticket to a cushy lifestyle. Herb doesn't even get to enjoy the lifestyle because he's always working so hard.

At this point in the story, Herb's just warming up. There's lots more woe to go when you're talking with Herb. Actually, it's not so much a two-way conversation as it is a one-way monologue of victimhood.

But Herb's capacity to wallow in the swamps of persecution and sadness has begun to shift into an even lower gear. For example, when talk of potential layoffs at his company began to swirl, Herb got even more freaked out than usual. At home, he became so convinced that his house was going to catch fire that he began sleeping on his first-floor couch—the best place from which to make a run for safety.

Herb's family has endured his irrational embrace of victimhood for so long that they finally have given in. They've concluded that Herb is beyond the point of no return, so they've made the necessary accommodations and enabling behaviors. In doing so, they have reinforced Herb's thinking and actions.

The worst part is that Herb's behaviors and attitudes are starting to rub off on his teenage son. A self-generated pressure cooker is no place to spend your adolescence. Being a teenager is hard enough without the added layer of adopting a victim mentality.

It's the oldest excuse in the book: "If only I had (fill in the blank), I could be happy." More money. Better friends. A bigger house. A nicer car. A boss who isn't such a jerk. Kinder neighbors. The list is endless—and for a very good reason.

None of these external things can ever fix the real problem: the person in the mirror.

By looking outward, constantly and exclusively blaming other people, things, or circumstances for your troubles, you're blocking the chance for any real, meaningful, lasting improvement and growth.

Your biggest issue—and, at the same time, your biggest chance to get lifted up to a better life—is you. People typically don't like to hear this sort of truth telling. It's much easier to point fingers, cast blame, and complain about the unfairness of it all.

Well, here's some more tough Love: life's not fair. But once you take personal responsibility for your actions, attitude, confidence, and willingness to sacrifice for other people's benefit—as well as your choice to take control of your own story—life doesn't need to be fair anymore.

Instead, life can become a place where you can at last be comfortable in your own skin. Life becomes a place where the issue of fairness becomes a non-issue, because fairness by its very definition requires that you constantly compare yourself with others. There's no need for that. There's no benefit to that. There's no time for that.

Take stock of your strengths, and build on them. Appreciate the sources of Love and hope and joy in your life, and cherish and protect them. See what—or who—is dragging you down, and get away from that source. Life's too short to be anything but happy.

The person in the mirror would agree. Have an honest talk with him or her. You'll see. Introspection like this can be painful, but it's the necessary first step in stripping away a victim mentality. Otherwise, we buy into these victim messages. They become a way of life. They become our story.

In a sick way, though, if you don't carry around all of that victim-based drama in our society today, somehow you're the oddball!

When we constantly look outward for someone or something to blame for our difficulties—or for some outside source to save and deliver us from our troubles—our aim will never be true or even close to the mark.

By blaming, we are not taking responsibility to figure out the real issue. We don't take time to search within, because we're too busy doing other stuff, looking for the magic pill to make all the clouds go away.

Think about this, though. I mean really think about it. Could there be a less rational approach to living a life of victory? Do champions blame other people for their setbacks and disappointments? Do champions sit, complain, and wait for somebody else to swoop in and solve all of their problems? Do champions give up—ever?

No, of course not! Champions deal with the here and now and live in a place called the real world, where every person takes responsibility for himself or herself. Where people realize that not every project, relationship, or idea will succeed smoothly, but where each person's active and positive involvement offers the best chance to make it so. Champions live in a place where taking responsibility also means reaching out for help when needed, not as a sign of surrender or failure, but as a means of achieving positive forward motion.

Those living with a victim mentality, on the other hand, accelerate their own downward spiral. Living helpless and hopeless is not really living—it can literally affect your health. Researchers have proven that one of the primary causes of illness is self-created stress—the kind of stress that self-proclaimed victims heap upon themselves. According to the Centers for Disease Control, in fact, 90% of all illness is stress-related.

Cellular biologist Dr. Bruce Lipton, a leader in the field of "new biology," examined in detail the processes by which cells receive information. The implications of his research have radically changed our understanding of life.

Lipton's research shows that genes and DNA do not control our biology. Instead, signals from outside the cell, including the energetic messages emanating from our positive and negative thoughts, control our DNA.

Lipton examined cells under the microscope. He found that healthy cells congregated in the middle, peacefully and comfortably co-existing in a shared space. But when he introduced a toxic cell, the healthy cells moved away. Lipton determined that cells in the body constrict and tighten under stress, making them more prone to sickness. When healthy, though, cells open up and are better able to thrive.

How we think, then, controls how our cells function, which has a direct effect on our physical health. Living as a victim, in other words, makes us sick. Again, that's not living as a champion.

The self-described victim would benefit by asking a simple question: What's the worst that could happen? He or she could lose everything? Should that happen, there would be nothing left to worry about.

Here's the thing: We say life is too much, there are too many commitments, no time to relax or unwind or get healthy. Nonsense. The hard, cold fact remains that we don't create enough space to make the time we complain we don't have. We have stuff, but we are surviving, not living or thriving. After all, who told us we needed to be running all day with nothing left at home for the kids or each other?

It's all self-imposed stress, caused by permitting ourselves to live as victims.

Once more, I speak from personal experience. On the verge of losing everything, my wife and I gained everything instead. In the first years of our marriage, my wife suffered a stroke, and the focus of our lives changed. We immediately understood what truly matters in life, and we realized the weight of the unnecessary baggage we'd been carrying around. That weight had to go, so we sold our house quickly, downsized—or "right-sized," as they say in business—so that we wouldn't capsize. We made enough from the sale of the house to restart somewhere else with the right balance between work and home, including the financial foundation to be comfortable.

The result offered us a fresh start, with the right mental attitude toward each other's needs, plans to create our family, a healthy view of the role of money in our lives, and a vision of the kind of future we wanted to enjoy. Today, even after a second stroke, my wife lives a full and healthy life, and we have a solid marriage with two great children.

It took the emotional equivalent of an earthquake, though, to force us to hit the reset button and cast off any vestiges of victimhood that threatened to overtake our lives.

A key is to recognize and repel what I call "emotional contagion." This is how you react to events and people in your life, based on your emotional baggage. Unfortunately, most people learn to react to situations out of Fear, holding onto bad patterns, even from prior generations. This is happening to Herb's teenage son described in the opening story of this chapter. Herb's victim story is affecting how his teenage son views his own story, with the accompanying negative behaviors.

It's up to each person to realize he or she doesn't want to live like this. Coming to this epiphany represents the first, and crucial, step in escaping from a victim mentality.

When you say to yourself, "I want to thrive wherever I am," and believe what you say, you open the door to healing, growth, and a champion's life. When all is said and done, self-generated pressure usually isn't even real—and if it is, it's not as bad as you anticipate.

The trouble is that we hold onto all the emotional junk. Studies have shown that anger can remain in our minds and our emotional makeup for up to five days. In other words, once you get angry, it can take five days for that boil to come back down to a simmer.

You may tell yourself, "Well, I usually only get mad once or twice a week." Even at that pace, your anger never truly subsides. The anger never goes away; it never leaves you, either at the psychological or physiological level.

Do you remember Lipton's evidence that how we think affects our cells and our health? Simply put, even if you only get angry once or twice a week, that still means you are always angry. Who would choose to live like that?

The message here is not that it's always bad to express anger. Sometimes that's the most appropriate response. But realizing the overlapping effect of repeated bursts of anger— even when they seemingly occur far apart—should cause us to consider the effects, and whether or not we want to pursue alternative options.

The trick is to look inward. Try to minimize the impact of external sources of stress. The only person you can truly control and influence consistently is you. The decisions you make about how to react to external impulses affect you most directly.

Here's some exciting news: As you become more positive, getting further and further from the life of a self-proclaimed victim, it helps other people at the same time. Even with startling effect.

Can you accept the hypothesis that a single person's energy, enlightenment, and capacity to Love can influence 90,000 other people? How about 750,000 other people? 10 million? 70 million?

Why not go for it all, and say that a single person's Love—defined as being as close to God consciousness as possible—can counterbalance and influence the entire world? Could you believe such a claim? Would name-dropping Jesus or Buddha change your mind?

Research conducted some years ago by psychiatrist, physician, and spiritualist, Dr. David Hawkins, described in his book, *The Eye of the I: From Which Nothing is Hidden*, asserts that this phenomenon is true.

According to Hawkins, the 13 percent of high-energy/high-Love/high-God consciousness people on the earth are necessary to counterbalance the 87 percent who aren't operating at quite that level. Not only that, says Hawkins, if the 13-to-87 percent ratio were to tumble significantly out of balance, the entire human population of the planet would self-destruct under its own negativity.

To me, this simply means that it's better to operate from a foundation of Love than of Fear.

Why did Pope Francis cause such an awakening of humility and service, not just within his own church, but also around the world? Why can a new CEO, who builds camaraderie and consensus from a platform of respect, lead the organization to new heights when a predecessor could not? Why do parents, who lead by loving example—between each other, and among all of their children—see their families prosper, no matter what's in the checkbook or the bank?

You know the answer. It's the simplest thing to say but sometimes hard to live. It's Love. All you need is Love, as

Lennon and McCartney wrote all those years ago in their Abbey Road studios in London. As I've said repeatedly in this book, living from a platform of Love, not Fear, makes all the difference.

This recovery has to start within. When I realized I didn't want to live angry anymore, I also realized I couldn't blame my father anymore. Instead of letting my story be one of resentment and bitterness, I worked to make it a story of joy and betterment. Easy to do? Not at all. Worth the effort? Absolutely, as proven every single day.

You can't control anything that anybody else does—that's why a positive story has to start with controlling yourself. I wouldn't have wished my story on anyone, but once I changed it, my dad changed his story too.

I realized my dad was doing what he thought was right as he raised me. I see it now as an initiation that makes me Fearless when dealing with families and situations as a therapist and coach. I've seen it all, which means I go in thriving to any situation. My cells speak it. Kids, even pets, can see it.

To escape from a victim mentality, we need to see what the real issue is. We need to look at what we want versus what we don't want. We need to offer forgiveness, which frees us from the emotional contagion referenced earlier in this chapter. We need to take responsibility for what happens in our life and stop blaming outside factors. And we need to be around people who are like-minded, which means some relationships need to go by the wayside.

Eagles flock with eagles, not pigeons, after all. This does not mean adopting a sense of superiority, however. Consider the example of Mother Teresa. She took on the crushing despair of the poor of Calcutta. By the world's standards, she had nothing. By her own standards, as established by her foundation of faith-based Love, she had everything.

We all share the journey. It's a constant process of getting better, living in more victory. It requires deliberate choices along the way. It helps to look for lubricators—whether in Scripture, positive affirmation, surrounding yourself with similar people, or a combination of them all. Adopting an active stance—taking personal responsibility to change your story to change your life—means applying a concerted effort, every day. It may be easier to live from a mostly reactive stance, but that is obviously and inarguably a far lesser choice.

When you choose to launch beyond merely surviving to an attitude of thriving, you live with an attitude of abundance. People who choose to thrive have extraordinary things happen every day. When you follow a path of Love and responsibility, miracles happen.

What we think about, we bring about. It's like a furnace: whatever you feed it, it will consume. People who thrive know what they want, go after it, cut a new path to it, and take responsibility for it. If you've always been reactive, if you've always lived with a victim mentality, it can be hard to get past those negative assumptions.

But here's the great news—it can be done. Stop being judgmental. Stop the faulty assumptions about your life and how outside forces affect it ultimately. Adopt a deeper internal relationship with yourself. Know, celebrate, and share yourself with others.

It all starts inside—emotionally, "cellularly," spiritually. Escape the victim mentality and begin living the life of the champion you truly are.

Chapter 6

THE LANGUAGE OF LIFE

When my son knew what to do, I knew the rest of us would be okay, too.

The Center for Victory has made trips to Kenya for the past few years, working with adults and young people there to help them grow spiritually and emotionally as they work to improve the quality of their lives. On one such trip, we suddenly found ourselves forced to live out the principles we had been discussing—and this occurrence truly tested all of us.

The hotel where we were staying looked and felt nothing like its advertisements. It was a hovel, with poor service and sub-par food. None of our group had been very impressed. It's not that we had expected a five-star resort, but even with moderate expectations, we felt disappointed and perhaps a little apprehensive.

While at breakfast the second morning of our stay, the hotel manager walked over to our group and unceremoniously evicted us from the hotel. He offered no explanation, nor permitted any dialogue with us. He wouldn't even let us pay. It was a matter of "Get out now and never come around here again."

Suffice it to say, we were flabbergasted. And not only that, we were suddenly without a place to stay, eat, or conduct our program.

Now, despite all of the ideas and strategies concerning living a life of victory that we had been sharing with our Kenyan friends the day before, getting kicked out of our hotel shook us. I'm sorry to admit that some of us in the group did not exactly practice what we had been preaching. Some of us instinctively became anxious, frightened, angry, confrontational, and emotional—and our negative response began to affect other members of our group and the guards who were there to protect us.

Clearly, something had to be done to alter the trajectory we had begun to follow. The story had to change.

So, I went up to a guard and said, "It's going to be all right," and the anxiety was released.

My son asked, "Dad, is this an example of finding opportunity in crisis?"

I answered, "Yes," and knew that we would be all right.

Our group started praying in the street, singing together, as people from the neighborhood joined the circle. Even a dog joined us. Before long, we learned that a hotel down the street was able to take all of us in—offering ample rooms, a conference center, and much better quality of food than we had been served at the first hotel. The dog followed us to the new facility, too, and became our mascot for the trip.

There was no panic, even though we might have been headed that way. As the leader of this group, the one responsible, and the person others counted on to figure things out and set an example, I refused to become nervous or upset. I just kept saying, "We'll figure it out. It's going to be okay."

By responding to the situation calmly and speaking positively, not reacting in an emotional or violent way, I influenced the event. It did turn out okay. This episode, perhaps more clearly and undeniably than any other in recent memory, proved that what you think—and the language you use to share your thoughts—becomes your reality.

Your brain has a reticular activating system (RAS). This system controls where your thoughts concentrate. It acts like a furnace or a wood burner. Your RAS will feed on whatever you give it. In other words, your RAS generates the instructions you give yourself. Those instructions—understood as the choices you make between differing options and attitudes—could not be more important in how you live your life.

Noticing the difference between Velcro and Teflon can help us understand how the mind works. Velcro, an amazing invention, performs well and reliably. Adapted from nature, Velcro can grab hold and not let go. Teflon, also an amazing invention, is the polar opposite of Velcro. Teflon enables things to slide right off of it. No resistance at all. Just zip! It's gone.

So why do I offer these observations about two consumer products? Because they have direct and precise correlations to how our minds work—and our minds control the quality of our lives.

Say you've had a wonderful day. No traffic on the way into work. The boss calls you in and says you've been promoted with a nice raise to come. You get home and take the family out to a great dinner at a fancy restaurant. Then you walk back to the car, only to find that you've been hit with a $200 parking ticket and a flat tire.

What do you obsess about? What sticks in your head? What turns into Velcro? The parking ticket and the flat tire. What slides right off? What becomes Teflon? The happy day that preceded all the trouble.

Experts estimate that we spend 85% of our waking moments focused on negative self-talk. It's easy to chalk that up to human nature, but I strongly disagree. We always have a choice about what we permit our minds to cling to or let slide off. The truest definition of "human nature" is that we are created for abundance, happiness, and Love-based relationships.

This reminds me of a fable. One evening, an old Cherokee told his grandson about a battle that goes on inside people. He said, "My son, the battle is between two 'wolves' inside us all. One is Evil: It is anger, envy, jealousy, greed, and arrogance. The other is Good: It is peace, Love, hope, humility, compassion, and faith."

The grandson thought about this for a while, and then asked his grandfather, "Which wolf wins?"

The wise old man simply replied, "The one you feed."

You can choose to let positive thoughts become the Velcro of your mind. The ones that stick. The negative stuff can slide, Teflon-like, right off. But you need to make the right choice. Your RAS needs to know which direction to take you.

You can think happy, positive thoughts, but if you don't feel them—if your thoughts can't get you into an emotional connection as well as an intellectual choice—then your life cannot truly change. It's an incomplete process. You can become stifled with ideas like, "I've made so many mistakes that I don't deserve to be happy." Your instructions must become your reality, as driven by your RAS.

The instructions you give your RAS will determine your mind's focus. The more you dwell on something—whether good or bad, positive or negative, real or imagined—the more you will focus on it. This applies to anything in life: marriage, kids, work, other people, you name it.

Programming your thinking affects both your subconscious and conscious mind, which function in clearly different modes. The subconscious mind does not filter, while the conscious mind does. For example, if you watch a horror movie late at night, your conscious mind ingests the scary details of the story. After you go to bed, your subconscious mind fills the void and creates new images with an even wider perspective.

Dr. Bruce Lipton, introduced in Chapter 4, has much to say about the power of the subconscious and conscious mind. In *The Biology of Belief,* Lipton explains how the two minds make a dynamic duo. For example, says Lipton, the conscious mind can focus on a specific point, perhaps a party you are attending on the weekend. Meanwhile—and simultaneously, your subconscious mind can be attending to a different task, perhaps pushing a lawnmower with a dangerous blade around safely. The subconscious mind manages this task even though you aren't consciously attending to it.

Lipton continues,

The two minds are truly a phenomenal mechanism, but here is how it can go awry. The conscious mind is the 'self,' the voice of our own thoughts. It can have great visions and plans for a future filled with love, health, happiness, and prosperity. While we focus our consciousness on happy thoughts, who is running the show? The subconscious. How is the subconscious going to manage our affairs? Precisely the way it was programmed. The subconscious mind's behaviors when we are not paying attention may not be of our own creation because most of our fundamental behaviors were downloaded without question from observing other people.

Lipton contends that nature did not intend the presence of the dual minds to be a weakness. Rather, this duality is potentially a wonderful advantage. Imagine what it would be like if we had parents and teachers who consciously served as positive life models, behaving humanely and constructively with everyone. Imagine our minds programmed with such healthy behaviors. If such were the case, Lipton says, "We could be totally successful in our lives without ever being conscious!"

Lipton is correct. But we all know that we have not been programmed by observing flawless parents and other adult role models along the way. That's why it remains a self-motivated assignment to tweak your own RAS and mindset actively, if you want to make a meaningful and positive difference in how you approach people, decisions, and behaviors.

When you change the way you think about things, the way you think about things changes. As it says in the book of Proverbs, "As a man thinketh in his heart, so is he." In practical terms, that means if you constantly tell yourself things are tough, that becomes your focus and experience.

The limits of your language are the limits of your world. Don't stay stuck in negative assumptions, such as "marriage is hard; relationships are hard; and/or business is bad."

Make the choice: Will you live with a victim or a victor mentality? Henry Ford said, "Whether you think you can, or you think you can't, you're right." He understood the power of your RAS on your life, even though he didn't call it by those terms.

Here's a main idea: Once you expand your language, you expand your world. This goes beyond just "the power of positive thinking." It is steering your mind with such dedication that you achieve feelings that are actually more positive.

This mindset is the difference between enabling and empowering.

Enabling means handouts, Fear-based thinking—a welfare mentality, living as a victim. Empowering, on the other hand, means enhanced self-worth, Love-based thinking—a workfare mentality, living as a victor.

Anything you complain about—or celebrate—repeatedly is what you intend (give yourself instructions) to produce. That's why you need to watch your language. This can be an enormous challenge to turn your thinking around, to retrain your RAS toward a positive outlook.

In our Center for Victory workshops, one of the first exercises entails me asking what people want. Most of the time, they begin answering that question by telling me everything they don't want. That's starting from Fear, from negativity, from a victim's mindset.

As Lipton describes, you create your being by understanding how your story has been formed and influenced by others along the way. Parents raise children to believe people are basically good or bad, and that's what their children will believe. Again, we become that which we focus on and become emotionally involved in.

On a microscale, people who have experienced trauma can't become emotionally involved with people again and slowly let themselves sink into depression. On a macroscale, we're told to Fear other cultures, leading to faulty assumptions that can explode into major conflicts. If it were the other way around, we could potentially avoid all war.

We see this phenomenon played out in the classroom, as well, where certain kids are labeled as either good or bad. As a result, the teacher's RAS will catch negative behaviors being manifested by the "bad" students, because the teacher is actively looking for them. These can be seriously faulty assumptions, however.

At one school, the rosters for special education and advanced placement students were reversed by mistake on the first day of classes, and the teachers didn't know. Each group of students lived up to those respective expectations. The special education kids worked hard and participated, while the AP kids misbehaved and slacked off—each group behaving as it did, taking its cue from the expectations of the teachers, who had assumed they would see what they saw.

We've talked a lot about changing your RAS, but not a lot about how to do it. Here are some thoughts on that.

First, find ways to slow down your brain. Most people live in a constant state of stress, which makes it difficult to alter the way your mind is trained and predisposed to think.

We all have alpha and beta brain waves. Alpha waves work during meditation, prayer, and regulation. Alpha waves move at a slower pace, making it easier to insert new ideas. Conversely, beta waves focus and complete school or work-based tasks easily. They are involved in conscious thought, and logical thinking. Beta waves tend to have a stimulating affect. Too much beta may lead to us experiencing excessive stress and/or anxiety, making it much more difficult for new ideas to break through.

This is why starting each day in prayer keeps us healthier. The healthy oxytocin generated during alpha wave-centric prayer time remains elevated when you're not dreading your day. Think about and anticipate the good things that are going to happen that day. Consider how many new friends you're going to make. You expand your physiology, your vibratory energy, when you approach your day this way.

Another way to reorient your RAS is to remain plugged into what I call the three A's:

- Awareness: Expanding knowledge and understanding

- Alignment: Getting lined up with the right people, watching your language

- Affirmation: Living a more positive, healthier, relationship-driven, and Love-based life

Remember that no one has ever gotten something good by worrying about it. Good things happen when you change the "real" of your life, and that requires changing your RAS, the way you think, the direction in which your life is directed naturally. You can't expect to change the external without changing the internal first, by literally creating the image you want in your mind.

Fear distorts that image, placing you in a state of not feeling good enough. Get rid of emotional contagion—the old "story" that's been holding you back—to achieve increased emotional flexibility. This sounds hard because it goes against everything you've been told in your life, but it can be done.

Start with the end in mind, like Arnold Schwarzenegger, who envisioned every chapter of his life long before it happened—from champion body builder to movie star to successful politician. Like Arnold, you may not know how it will happen, and you don't have to know how it will happen, but you must have complete trust that it will. Why? Because your mind will believe, focus, and act on it.

Ponder this central question: What's your assignment on earth? Whatever it is, believe that you are genetically accurate and emotionally equipped to achieve it. Whatever you're supposed to do, you're to do it in a great way.

Scripture says so, and so does your own mind. You just have to dig deep enough to discover it.

Remember, there's no such thing as a loser—just a person who's lost. Get your thinking and your language straight, and you won't be lost any more.

Chapter 7

ACHIEVING THE NECESSARY AWARENESS

Looking out the clear ceiling-to-floor window of his corner office, Ross the Boss could see Tony, and it made him uncomfortable.

Ross had risen to the head of sales for the company, and knew how the job was done. You kept a roster of prospects, you got to know the names of their spouses and kids, you sent birthday cards, you kept a tickler file, touched base just regularly enough to remain top-of-mind, and you knew your products like nobody's business. A proven formula, never known to fail.

His polished chrome desk, view of downtown out spacious office windows, and the team of hard chargers out on the sales floor provided unassailable proof that Ross's way was the best way to generate impressive numbers for the company.

Not just the best way, thought Ross. The only way.

That's what made his observance of Tony so troublesome. Tony had a different style to his sales. He worked a lot more loosely. He had no formal system in play. He used that silly social media too much.

Tony struck Ross as a boy role-playing in a man's world.

The only trouble with this assessment? Tony's sales stood at twice the total of the next highest person on Ross' staff.

The executives upstairs were delighted with the results, of course. But couldn't they see the real issue? Tony may be getting sales out the wazoo, but he was doing it wrong! This couldn't possibly continue. Tony's performance was simply unsustainable, unremarkable, and inexcusable.

No matter how many times Ross tried to mentor, redirect, and correct him, Tony just wouldn't listen. In Ross's little stable of sales studs, Tony was a wild bronco who could not—no, would not—be broken and tamed.

There could be only one solution. Tony had to go. Ross called him in to his chrome-plated office, asked Tony for his employee ID, called in Human Resources to make it official, and tossed Tony out onto the street.

Now, at last, Ross could relax, knowing that the remainder of his sales team would all be doing things the right way. His way. Or else they'd be following Tony out the door.

Instead, six months later, the company fired Ross.

Sales had tanked. It seemed there was more than one way to get the job done, after all.

Ross the Boss had no idea how he came across. He operated in an awareness vacuum. Proud, haughty, imperious, unbending, and ignorant. What's worse, this lack of awareness prevented him from even considering the possibility of being wrong—or, at the very least, misinformed. Such awareness could have opened the door to positive change and improvement.

Every instance of growth entails some element of pain. A seed gets planted in the dark ground and must split open, fight its way upward, and eventually crack through the surface, drawing nourishment from water and sunlight to yield its fruit. A mother must endure incredible assaults to her body during labor to give birth to a child. And each person must face the truth about his or her attitudes, assumptions, behaviors, and their consequences, before deciding to pursue meaningful change.

So, if we're in a not-so-good place, how do we get unstuck? It's a genuine challenge because while we're taught that we may need to choose a different route, we're not taught to identify what keeps us stuck where we are.

You can read all sorts of books on what constitutes a good diet. Hours of TV infomercials offer their own brand of help, too. You can intellectually research and absorb ideas on how to become more fit and eat in a healthier way, but if every time you get stressed you reach for the Ho-Hos, what's the point?

Making meaningful change requires more than an intellectual exercise. It also takes an emotional commitment. You need more than information. You need to be aware. There's a difference between the two. The brain needs information. The heart needs awareness.

Choice is a direct function of awareness. If you're not aware, you can't choose. That was Ross the Boss's problem. As

I've said in earlier chapters, as human beings we are hard-wired for connection. But if we do things to push people away, like Ross did with Tony, we're not aware and that connection cannot happen.

If we're not aware of the nuggets we've put together, the many events large and small that comprise our story, we can be brought down or up easily. For example, the addict doesn't start out with the express intent of becoming an addict. A series of bad decisions, bad luck, and bad associates brings him or her to that tragic place. Similarly, some people can't see themselves as champions and have no aspiration to become one. They wonder: Can I live up to my latest success? Can I handle the pressure of doing well?

In the holiday classic, *It's a Wonderful Life*, the sinister banker, Mr. Potter, offers the hero of the story, George Bailey, the chance to join his organization for lots more money and a much more comfortable life than George currently has. When George balks at the offer, Potter exclaims, "Confound it, man! Are you afraid of success?" Many people are afraid of success, because change means some pain and discomfort.

My own story reflects this fact. For years, in college and beyond, I reacted to other people in a continuously defensive manner. I was brusque and dismissive, sometimes shouting, and occasionally violent. I'm not particularly proud of this part of my life, and I've put it behind me, for the better.

I had a dawning awareness that my pattern of interacting and reacting to other people was actually a repetition of the way I had always reacted to my dad. This led to the stunning realization that I was still acting as a victim. Until that awareness crashed onto my brain and into my heart, making any kind of change from that pattern would have been impossible or insufficient at best.

Changing your story changes your reactions. The task becomes replacing your program, your story, with something different. What are the triggers? For starters, stop seeing disagreement or disharmony as a crisis. Resist the temptation to run to the worst-case scenario. Consciously seek moderation. Look deeper inside to find that part of you that wants a level-set, a balanced life. Find your internal reset button.

Remember that the things we react to most strongly are the things we don't understand. We have no frame of reference around them. We're flying blind, which makes it easy to crash. We've all heard of lottery winners and young athletes signing huge professional contracts only to blow through their newfound riches quickly because they don't have the right program. They lack the awareness needed to steward those funds responsibly. They make bad decisions. They need a temperature check from trusted people around them; otherwise, they come to resent themselves for squandering their good fortune.

The saddest part of all this? We all set ourselves and each other up for such failures. We're told to not talk to strangers, to be seen and not heard, to not bite off more than we can chew. Life isn't meant to be that hard! It's meant to be abundant, but we make it difficult.

Because of this faulty societal programming, people resist changing parts of themselves, for Fear they will lose themselves in the process. Yet the ramifications of this reluctance and avoidance of making positive change exacerbates the problem.

We become addicted to stress. We can't relax, even on vacation. Have you seen grown men and women, sitting under beach umbrellas on gorgeously sunny summer days, checking their smartphones for e-mails, texts, and Facebook posts—

missing time with their children and wasting an opportunity to plug into their own refresh and regeneration time?

To continue with the seasonal example, in the Northeast U.S. where my home and company are based, winter can be tough. Most seasons, we don't get a walloping huge snow dump all at once. That would be tough enough to cope with. No, instead we get an inch one day, then two inches the next day, then another inch the day after that. Those day-after-day increments wear on you. The snow never seems to go away. The relentlessness of it bothers people.

The same thing happens with our relationships, the decisions we make, and the actions we take. As I mentioned in an earlier chapter, studies show that anger can remain in your mind and your emotional makeup for up to five days. Anger can be like that day-after-day snowfall, never going away, never leaving you, either at the psychological or physiological level.

It would be inappropriate and unrealistic to vow never to get angry. Sometimes anger is the healthiest response. But it's important to be aware of the overlapping effects of repeated bursts of anger. When you habitually react with anger to external impulses, the person who gets the most hurt is you.

The solution begins with greater awareness. Making a change to a destructive pattern can be difficult, but you can do it, and the benefits will far outpace and outlast any pain you experience in the process.

Unfortunately, it can be a lot easier to play the victim than to change. I once knew a person who constantly talked about how sick she was. Everything hurt. No one could help her feel better, and worse, no one seemed to care about her suffering.

This relentless narrative—regardless of what percentage of it happened to be true—had two damaging effects. First, the habit eventually rubbed off on this woman's children. This is a sad parental legacy, to say the least. Second, no one wanted to be around any of them because all their company represented was complaining and pleas for sympathy. As people bluntly avoided them, it seemed to reinforce the victimhood mentality and made the situation worse.

The drama—does anybody really need it? Can you fit in without a good victim story? Yes, I say! Yes! Playing the victim equates with upside-down thinking, yet that's precisely how we have set up expectations in this society.

Here's my take on the matter. Yes, bad things happen every now and then, but we don't have to reinforce them constantly. To do so only prevents us from achieving the awareness required to make lasting, positive, meaningful change.

When we constantly rehearse the bad things, we can get sucked into a whirlpool that's very tough to escape. One of the unerring truths of life is that when we are stressed, we regress. As the little annoyances start to bubble up and cluster into big irritants, we have the tendency to blow our tops. Not only does this preclude a mature, rational approach to problem solving, it exacerbates any situation.

When you're in a hole, stop digging. When you see a fire, don't throw gasoline on it. When the guy with the football has been tackled, don't pile on top after the whistle blows. Pick your cliché or metaphor, but you get the idea. Reflecting on how people let stress steer them into a regressed mindset, I think of George Costanza from the *Seinfeld* series. In nearly every episode, life found a way to frustrate George into some level of frenzy, tizzy, and explosive outburst.

In one memorable story, Jerry was at a dealership looking to get a new car while George tagged along for moral support. Hungry from missing lunch, George spent the entire episode trying—and failing—to find something to eat. He just missed the last of the free donuts in the customer lounge, his Twix bar got stuck in the vending machine, and he became convinced that a mechanic came in after him and stole it. Near the end of the show, George emits a primal howl to the universe in utter exasperation. He has completely regressed to the level of a shouting infant in a playpen!

Stress is, was, and always will be the number one obstacle to building and maintaining a healthy, Love-based life. It does nasty things to us physiologically as well as psychologically. Stress limits thinking and reason. The *Seinfeld* episode above treats it for laughs, but stress can actually become quite serious, even dangerous.

Look for ways to eliminate the sources of stress from your life. Think intentionally about how you react to situations, and choose to avoid stress. It takes a determined effort and lots of practice, but if you don't want to regress, you must limit your stress. And, as we've been emphasizing in this chapter, that turnaround begins with a greater awareness and acknowledgement of the sources of stress.

Put another way, you must take your story, view it clearly, understand how it affects you and how others see you, and be responsible for it. I wouldn't have wished my childhood on anybody, but if I hadn't gone through my childhood and taken responsibility for it, I couldn't do what I do today.

I realized I had changed my story—after realizing that my treatment of people was reflecting my interaction with my dad—when I noticed that my fingernails had begun growing again. I had chewed them down my whole life from the stress, anger, and frustration I felt growing up. It took a physical manifestation like growing fingernails to help me see that I had achieved the necessary awareness, turned the corner, and left that undesirable behavior behind.

Don't be afraid to re-examine your story. You may not want to confront it again, but you must. When you don't confront your story, it creates unconscious stress. You can't live the life of a champion like that. Remember, you can do anything, but only with unconditional Love for yourself. Nothing else matters or is possible without it.

Consider this question: If you were guaranteed not to fail, what could you achieve? The answer is "anything." Why? Because in a successful, balanced, happy, healthy life, Love always wins over Fear. Responsibility always wins over casting blame. We need to embrace victory, believing that great people are always going to come into our lives. Each morning, we need to believe it's going to be a great day. That our family members are great.

Hold the paradigm that everything's going to be okay, because it is. When you stay in awareness, don't let ego take over, because all ego wants is to be fed constantly. In truth, experiencing tough times can bring us together and not push us apart. In fact, tough moments are the ones in which we need each other more than ever, even though our society may seem to value the self-sufficient loner more.

In all things, we need to be authentic. Be who you are, then give people around you permission to do the same. Of the many memorable lines from the 1989 film *Dead Poets Society*, the English professor (played by Robin Williams) offers this thought to his impressionable class of young men:

> *We don't read and write poetry because it's cute. We read and write poetry because we are members of the human race. And the human race is filled with pas-*

sion. And medicine, law, business, engineering, these are noble pursuits and necessary to sustain life. But poetry, beauty, romance, love, these are what we stay alive for. To quote from Whitman, 'O me! O life!... of the questions of these recurring; of the endless trains of the faithless...of cities filled with the foolish; what good amid these, O me, O life?' Answer. That you are here—that life exists, and identity; that the powerful play goes on and you may contribute a verse. What will your verse be?"

We all carry our own life story around with us. For some people, that story becomes a sack full of chains and weights and regrets and Fears and self-loathing. A ton of baggage with no wheels can become tough to carry around, adding frustration and resentment that—like accumulated interest on a bank loan that is added to principal, generating even more interest—only makes the load heavier in the end.

Conversely, other people's stories can be light, in both weight and appearance. Filled with gratitude, hope, Love, and optimism, these stories not only are easier to carry, but are meant to be shared and emulated.

Here's the secret: No one's story has to be such a downer. Yes, bad stuff happens. But, as the English professor whispered to his wide-eyed students, "The powerful play goes on...and you may contribute a verse. What will your verse be?"

What will your story be? It's always up to you. You may be going through tough times, but the good news is that you're going through them. You don't have to carry them around on your back forever. They don't have to be your story. Achieve awareness and make the change. Refuse to let Fear and pessimism master you. Look for the reasons human beings stay alive. Live for Love. That's the story we all are meant to tell the world.

We have a tendency to make living day-to-day way too complicated, when the essence of happiness, peace, balance, and joy remains—always—in plain view, and it's so simple. Will you live based on Love, or based on Fear? That's what Scripture says, all through the Old and New Testaments. That's where the central messages of all major religions agree. That's what wise philosophers and spiritual gurus have held to be true for centuries.

Living a Love-based life means accepting yourself and others. It means seeing the good, the positive, and the hopeful in every person, every circumstance, and every possibility. It means holding onto a faith in something bigger than yourself and using that faith as the springboard to a happy life, free from undue, unhelpful, and unnecessary anxiety. Love lets you live each day fresh, with a happy and grateful heart. Living a life based on Fear, naturally, produces the opposite effects. Fear steals hope, and when there's no hope, there can be no peace.

We are not born with limitations. We are all about empowering people to live as victors, not enabling people to live as victims.

Here is what leads to victory: We must have the courage to discover our true selves at this time and place, to achieve the needed awareness as the first step in changing for the better. The goal is simply to be the best "you" possible. If everyone did this, can you imagine how much smoother, happier, more enjoyable, rewarding, and successful life would be?

When you do not allow negativity to grow, it has nowhere to go. The only thing preventing you from healthy relationships is Fear. When you throw Fear down, it's gone, and you have a clear shot at being the best you possible.

I've always appreciated this passage by Marianne Williamson, from her book, *A Return to Love: Reflections on the Principles of a Course in Miracles.* See if it speaks to you the same way.

> *Our deepest fear is not that we are inadequate. Our deepest fear is that we are powerful beyond measure. It is our light, not our darkness that most frightens us. We ask ourselves, Who am I to be brilliant, gorgeous, talented, and fabulous? Actually, who are you not to be? You are a child of God. Your playing small does not serve the world. There is nothing enlightened about shrinking so that other people will not feel insecure around you. We are all meant to shine, as children do. We were born to make manifest the glory of God that is within us. It is not just in some of us; it is in everyone and as we let our own light shine, we unconsciously give others permission to do the same. As we are liberated from our own fear, our presence automatically liberates others.*

Growth always entails some level of pain. Work for awareness to start the process. The change to come is well worth it.

Chapter 8

EMOTIONAL FLEXIBILITY

The young man, barely into his teens, sat defiantly on the stage of one of those awful, dreadful, shameful afternoon TV shows that puts every undesirable trait known to the American public on display—for a public that, sadly, can't seem to get enough of it.

The kid's father took off before the kid had even been born. The mother barked at the smarmy host that she did the best she could with what she had to work with, which wasn't much. No money, no husband, no help. And trying to raise this good-for-nothing kid all by herself. It sure wasn't easy, and she wasn't done yet. He had barely started high school, and it would be a miracle if he ever graduated, she taunted.

Spurred on by the leering, cheering studio audience, the mother gained courage and momentum to continue the attack. She recounted every blunder and mistake her kid had ever made, proclaiming each offense at the top of her voice. Every instance of his stupidity and arrogance got shouted, greeted by more cheers.

With each declaration out of his mother's mouth, the young man sunk a little lower into his seat, but his facial expression only became more angry, sullen, and spiteful. It looked as though he was about to explode at any moment—which, of course, the people in the studio, along with the host, couldn't wait to see.

After a few minutes of this public humiliation, the host unveiled the coup de grace. A youth boot camp drill sergeant strode out from behind the set, marched right up to the young man, made him stand at attention, and commenced berating him mercilessly until, at last, the kid finally responded.

He didn't shout back. He didn't storm off. He used the only tool left to defend himself and still hang onto some shred of dignity and self-respect.

The young man began to cry. His soul, he must have decided, deserved better than what he was getting.

Beyond the cruelty, beyond the shaming, beyond the indefensible actions of the so-called adults in this scenario, lurk some bigger, deeper questions:

- How does a relationship sink to this depth?
- Is reacting emotionally to situations the only option?
- When, if ever, is it okay to relinquish control over our relationships?
- How does a response differ from a reaction, and why might a response be better?

The secret lies in emotional flexibility—utilizing the knowledge and strength not to *react* to the irrational or uncharitable behaviors of others, but instead to *respond* to them in ways that both preserve your dignity and model a better approach to others. But let's not sugarcoat this. Shifting from a default mode of reacting to one of responding can be one of the toughest challenges of your life.

Why? Because our society has drilled an expectation of emotional reactivity into our brains. A natural question, then, might follow: Aren't I supposed to react to behavior that hurts or offends me? Answer: No, because reacting to undesirable behavior only spawns more undesirable behavior.

All emotional reactivity comes from unfinished business. When I react to someone, I enable him or her to continue to act in the same pattern. I become responsible for that person's behavior. I grant permission for that behavior to continue. Put it this way: By escalating the volume of your voice and the level of your anger to that of the person who's provoking you, all you do is drop to that person's level. The situation doesn't get better; it gets worse.

Would you ever try to put your wife or your husband into a behavior-management program? Probably not. So why do parents try to do this to a child? Or supervisors to employees? All this realistically does is create more work for the parent or supervisor, because from that point on, the child or the employee has free reign to blame the parent or supervisor for any subsequent behavior. Reacting ineffectively or trying to clamp others too tightly doesn't do anything to create relationships. Just the opposite. Because reactivity breeds more reactivity, and reactivity—just like radioactive uranium in a nuclear reaction—can build and truly mess you up.

Brain studies reveal that pathways—grooves in the gray matter—get established for different types of thoughts, feelings, and responses. The brain's pathways created for Love, peace, and happiness, however, aren't used as much as the ones for Fear, conflict, and anxiety. This is because whatever we do more often, or whatever makes a stronger impression on our lives gets reinforced more deeply.

You can blame your prehistoric ancestors for this. When a saber-toothed tiger or a tyrannosaurus rex might be salivating just around the next rock, waiting to devour an ancestor, that sense of alarm, Fear, and violence crowded out any effects of a relaxing evening in the cave with the kids. We have been conditioned for centuries to reinforce this reactive state.

Parents and society both tell us to hold our emotions within. This inhibits healthy relationships. Makes sense, doesn't it? After all, who wants to be around someone when he or she is emotionally reactive? And reactivity also inhibits our health. When we react emotionally, the state of our very cells gets affected. They constrict, they slow down, they don't function as designed, and this can easily cause health problems. On the other hand, when we avoid reacting, and instead respond emotionally in a positive way, open, robust, healthy cells result.

When I work with individuals, groups, and families, we talk about the challenges of transitioning from emotional reaction to emotional response. Here are the four main challenges:

1. UNLEARNING THE BAD STUFF

It's socially acceptable to react to anger with anger, but that's not the optimal decision. Anger is a primary emotion, really rooted in Fear. We react with anger because we Fear where the situation could lead next.

When you remain emotionally flexible and choose to respond, and not react, you have a much better idea of where the situation is headed—at least from your perspective. By not permitting yourself to get sucked into the cyclone of sarcasm, insults, or intimidation swirling around another person, you retain control of the situation. You keep your peace.

Jesus knew the wisdom of this approach. In the Sermon on the Mount as described in Matthew, Jesus said, "Blessed are the merciful, for they will be shown mercy," and, "Blessed are the peacemakers, for they will be called children of God," and later, "You have heard that it was said, 'An eye for an eye and a tooth for a tooth.' But I say to you, offer no resistance ..."

So, how do you become more emotionally flexible? By following the wise words of Mahatma Gandhi, who said, "Be the change you wish to see in the world." Put another way, look for examples to follow, and then lead by example to help others do the same.

Know where you're starting from and know what kind of life you want to have moving forward. Your paradigm is inseparable from your character, but your paradigm can always change, expand, and improve. But never forget that you need to do the hard work yourself. Remember those brain pathways—dig some deeper trenches related to Love, patience, empathy, and peace.

In an earlier chapter, we talked about Teflon and Velcro in the brain. The good stuff tends to slide off like Teflon while the bad stuff sticks like Velcro. You need to even the odds, at least, by making a conscious effort every day to register and record the positive people and events in your brain pathways. That gives the positives at least a fighting chance of being retained internally. You must establish a level playing field in your mind.

When you stop reacting, you create more time for you. Those silly, useless, nobody-wins battles go away when you respond, and not react, emotionally. Taking the anger out of interactions also takes the personalization out of it. The un-conditional person—the one with emotional flexibility, who responds and not reacts—causes bad behavior to stop, while the reactive person reinforces it. Unlearn that conditioned fallback position. You'll be happier for it.

2. STOPPING CONDITIONS ON RELATIONSHIPS

Here's another faulty assumption that has been a societal norm for far too long. Soothing and healing can only come from things. Baloney! Don't you believe this, even though you've probably had the message hammered into you since birth. Watch television for more than 15 minutes, and you'll hear how you can't possibly live with yourself unless you have *this* car, or *those* shoes, or *that* teeth whitener.

Good grief. What a damaging and dangerous way to live and to think about ourselves.

Healthy relationships—including the one we have with ourselves—don't come with strings attached. There are no conditions.

When we allow things and superficial activities to fill the gaps where healthy relationships should be, it can lead to addictive behavior. At its core, addiction is an external attempt to address internal distress. We can delve into work, to the exclusion of the people who are most important to us. Exercise can become an obsession, actually damaging a person's health. Seemingly good, positive things can cause emotional damage because they're grounded in conditions. The unspoken thought, "I love you if..." usually leads to trouble.

As I've said throughout this book, as human beings created in the image of the Almighty, we are hardwired to connection. "Love one another as I have loved you," Christ told his disciples. No strings attached. Free, full, and open—that's how healthy connections and healthy relationships should function. Emotional flexibility makes it possible.

3. ESCAPING THE DRAMA OF A VICTIMHOOD MENTALITY

Archie Bunker, in the old *All in the Family* TV series, once exclaimed, "I ain't paranoid! Why is everybody against me?"

Yeah, everyone's against you. Keep telling yourself that and eventually you'll be unable to believe anything else. Reinforcing a life story of victimhood creates disempowerment, a sense of entitlement (that you're owed something), and a mentality of blame that makes everybody but you responsible for your life. It's a dead end if you have any hope of living a life of victory.

In the U.S., we have 6% of the world's population and 80% of the world's attorneys. And for a very simple reason. Too many people in this country enjoy playing the victim. It's so much easier to offload responsibility, to throw up your hands and throw in the towel. To quit trying, start crying, and put the blame on somebody else.

You don't believe that a mentality of victimhood pervades our society? Do you remember the woman who won millions from McDonald's after filing a lawsuit alleging that the restaurant served her coffee that was too hot? People sue tobacco companies over developing lung cancer from a lifetime of smoking. They sue fast-food chains for making their kids obese, after hitting the drive-through window four times a week. Have we all gone crazy? Who made anyone light a cigarette? Pound mayo-soaked hamburgers down our kids' throats?

Can't people accept responsibility for themselves anymore? I've noticed also that people who feel comfortable as victims tend to congregate around others who think the same way. Victims attract other victims. So be careful whom you talk to and hang around with because a victim's story doesn't have to be your story.

The emotionally flexible person challenges and marginalizes victimization by accepting personal responsibility for his or her choices. It requires a sober, honest process of self-examination. Are your relationships healthy or not? Do they build up the people involved or tear them down, tear them apart? What does your future look like? Being a victim gives your future away while standing up and standing out puts your future back into your hands.

Most accomplished people have had experiences that could have left them a victim, not victors—as bitter, not better. As I mentioned earlier, Oprah was abused sexually as a child. Bill Clinton's biological father died in a car crash before the future president was born, and his stepfather was an alcoholic who abused Clinton's mother on occasion. The world is filled with people who chose to overcome their negative heritage, accept responsibility for their own lives, and achieve success beyond even their own expectations.

You can choose not to live as a victim. I know, because I made that choice. My childhood, as described in the introduction to this book, was difficult, sad, and even dangerous at times. But there came a moment of clarity.

At the moment of my own personal epiphany, I decided to stop living in Fear and anger and resentment, and instead to live a life based on Love, acceptance, and understanding. And do you know something? When I made the decision to change my story in this way, an unexpected but wonderful thing soon followed.

My dad's life changed, too. Our stories changed together, and today he is my best friend, my trusted confidante, and the greatest grandfather you'd ever want to meet. Our experience proves that as you unlock your best "you," you give other people permission to do the same.

Misery may enjoy company, but when you turn it around, so does joy. Passion and courage are contagious. Bad stuff happens to everybody, but it doesn't have to last forever. It doesn't need to become your story. Everybody is not out to get you. Everybody wants to be accepted, welcomed, understood, and Loved. Model those attributes and watch your world change for the better.

4. KEEPING AT IT!

The change I'm talking about doesn't always come easy. It takes practice to move from a life of reacting to a life of responsibility. Achieving emotional flexibility takes a dedicated, focused, determined effort—because we have been programmed by society to act in exactly the opposite way.

When the transition succeeds, though, the benefits last a lifetime. You move from trying to assert constant control over other people to using your example to influence and inspire them. You naturally offer and encourage more give and take, rather than insisting that others accept your ideas. It becomes second nature to look for the win-win scenario, where everyone comes out feeling good about a relationship or interaction. You look for positive solutions, instead of punishments and retribution.

This way of living, in which you actively and eagerly strive for greater purpose and significance—both for your own life and as benefit to the lives of others—starts with you and must stay with you.

So here's the first step to take on this lifelong pursuit of greater emotional flexibility: Create your personal mission statement. Mine is a very short, yet powerful, one:

To live a life of Love.

Working to conduct my life each day according to that ideal has made all the difference to me, the people closest to me whom I Love, my friends and business associates, and possibly even some people I'm not even aware of. It takes a daily commitment. Yet it has proven, repeatedly, to be the most important decision I've ever made. You can experience that same kind of reward, and today is the day to begin.

Make the choice to sow Love, not Fear. Be emotionally flexible. Unlearn bad habits, false assumptions, and negative behaviors. Foster relationships with no strings attached. Step away from a victim mentality and take personal responsibility for your life. And never, ever give up.

Chapter 9

CONCLUSION

Let me again pose the question I asked at the start of this book—Are you crazy?

Are you crazy to accept a life with little control over its future, nagging negative thoughts affecting your relationships, an undercurrent of Fear, and a lack of true joy and peace? I'd have to say, "Yes," to that one.

Are you crazy to want to learn and grow, shifting your focus to building healthy relationships based on Love? I'd give that one a resounding, "No."

Through my personal story seen at the beginning of the book, along with the true stories at the start of each chapter, I've tried to illustrate how people can choose the path of their lives. I've tried to show how each person's past "story" can define him or her for years, or how that person can rewrite that story, actively and intentionally, for the better.

Life's an interesting journey. With the peaks, you're going to have to get through some valleys. Not much anybody can do to change that basic fact. But you always—always—have the choice about how you will view, interpret, and deal with the highs and lows certain to come your way. You can—and should, deserve to, and will—live a life of victory.

The essence comes down to a single, simple idea. It is simple to say but a challenge to live out. Choose Love over Fear. Know who you are, and if you don't like your own picture, change it. Accept in your heart that you are beautiful, wonderful, and entitled to a life brimming over with happy, healthy relationships. Once you know this in your heart, your mind will follow.

I know this approach works because it's my story, as well.

Knowing what anger and sorrow feels like has enabled me to be empathetic toward the people I counsel. Sharing that same frame of reference—but, as important, serving as living proof that you can change permanently for the better—provides the foundation for healing and growth.

All of us are wired for connection. When you are the truest, best, "you," that person helps to create a better world, through each healthier relationship. You create better people around you by internally motivating them.

I discovered the following poem in a book my dad had on his bookshelf, *Think and Grow Rich*, by Napoleon Hill, published around the time of the Great Depression. We use it to close out our live interactive workshops at the Center for Victory. I think it sums up much of what I have intended to share with you in this book.

THE VICTOR

If you *think* you are beaten, you are,
    If you *think* you dare not, you don't.
If you like to win, but *think* you can't,
    It's almost certain you won't.

If you *think* you'll lose, you're lost.
    For out in the world we find,
Success begins with a fellow's will—
    It's all in the *state of mind.*

If you *think* you are outclassed, you are,
    You've got to *think* high to rise.
You've got to be *sure of yourself* before
    You can ever win the prize.

Life's battles don't always go
    To the stronger or faster man,
But sooner or later, the man who wins
    Is the man WHO THINKS HE CAN!

We're all called to live in a spirit of joy, happiness, and Love. We're all called to be divine. To be well. To live the life of victory.

About the Author

Eric Guy, MSW, LSW, is a licensed social worker and internationally acclaimed speaker. As the founder of Center for Victory, Eric works with individuals and organizations across the country and around the world to help them unlock their personal potential and achieve their greatest success.

In his role as Chief Victory Officer, Eric designs and facilitates training and retreats to assist families, educators, mental health providers, and business professionals to discover and embrace their personal genius and the power of their relationships. He also provides customized programming in the form of intensive in-home treatment and individualized coaching.

Through his extensive work in the social services field, Eric has discovered how powerful our subconscious minds can be. This understanding has led him to work with clients to unlock the potential that their subconscious has suppressed. Once the power of the subconscious is released, Eric guides his clients through a process that unlocks their personal and professional potential.

Eric has a keen and powerful ability to facilitate better ways of dealing with the external environment and conditioning while helping his clients embrace their personal genius, reduce stress, and eliminate barriers that create limits on their personal and professional satisfaction.

Eric has been a guest on many radio and television programs and is currently working on projects in Africa and South America.

Visit Us at Center for Victory

Center for Victory is a champion for individuals who seek ultimate success. Just as a champion guides, inspires, and pushes athletes to break barriers, Center for Victory unlocks, reinforces, and enriches the relationships of individuals, families, and leaders. This creates meaningful success in life, family, and business.

Our true selves—which lie beneath our conscious thoughts and actions—power our connection with others and define who we are. That's why self-awareness, personal growth, healing, and achievement must begin with an understanding of ourselves and our relationships with others.

Our professional team:

- Provides unique counseling, presentations, and retreat experiences that enable you to eliminate the gaps between the true person you are and the way you lead your daily life.

- Empowers you to create better ways for yourself and your loved ones to evaluate, learn, heal, and ultimately lead the successful life you want.

- Gives you the tools to become a better neighbor, worker, parent—and above all else, PERSON.

At Center for Victory, we've successfully guided thousands of clients on their journey to greater success. Explore our website, and then contact us to learn how Center for Victory can help you to achieve ultimate success in your life, family, and business.

To contact the author, Eric Guy, visit:

Website .... : www.CenterForVictory.com

Email .... : Eric@CenterForVictory.com

LinkedIn .... : https://www.linkedin.com/in/ericguylsw

Twitter.......... : https://twitter.com/center4victory

Facebook..... : https://www.facebook.com/CenterforVictory/

YouTube ...... : https://www.youtube.com/watch?v=3KArK6Wrk30

Instagram .... : @CenterForVictory

Made in the USA
Columbia, SC
26 November 2018